In Search of Coffee Mountains

Elin Toona Gottschalk

In Search of Coffee Mountains

Drawings by Lotukata

Kestrel Books

Kestrel Books
Published by Penguin Books Ltd
Harmondsworth, Middlesex, England

First published in U.S.A. by Thomas Nelson Inc in 1977
This revised edition first published in Great Britain in 1979
ISBN 14 0 07226 54979
Filmset in Great Britain by
Northumberland Press Ltd, Gateshead, Tyne and Wear

Printed in Great Britain by offset lithography by
Billing & Sons Ltd, Guildford, London and Worcester

I dedicate this book with love
to my mother
and to my grandmother

Contents

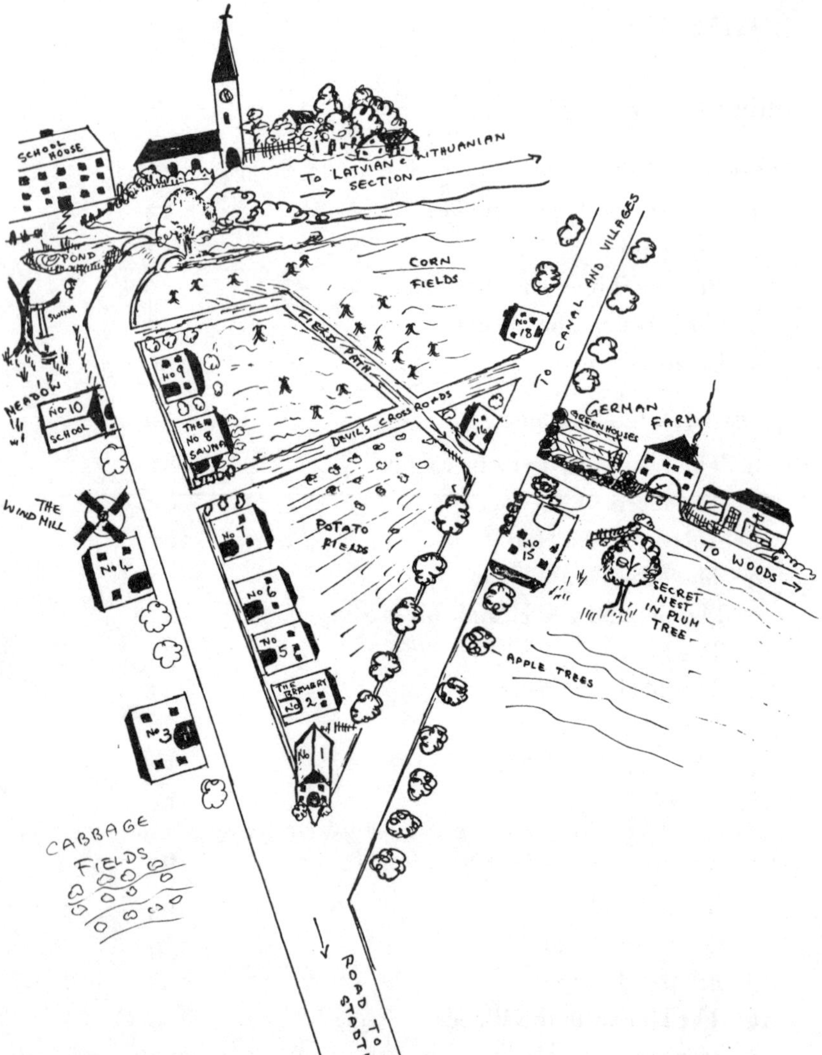
SCHOOL HOUSE
TO LATVIAN & LITHUANIAN SECTION
POND
SWING
CORN FIELDS
FIELD PATH
No 18
TO CANAL AND VILLAGES
MEADOW
No 9
No 10 SCHOOL
THE No 8 SAUNA
DEVIL'S CROSS ROADS
No 16
GERMAN FARM
GREEN HOUSES
THE WIND MILL
No 7
POTATO FIELDS
No 15
TO WOODS
No 4
No 6
SECRET NEST IN PLUM TREE
No 5
APPLE TREES
THE BREWERY No 2
No 3
No 1
CABBAGE FIELDS
ROAD TO STADTHAGEN

Author's note

In this book, I am describing life as I saw it in a Displaced Persons (DP) Camp in Germany, after the Second World War.

Estonia, where I was born, is the northernmost of the three Baltic States south of the Gulf of Finland. Estonians are linguistically related to the Finns and the Hungarians (the Finno-Ugrian group). Over the centuries, Estonia was occupied by Germany, Sweden and Russia.

After the Russian Revolution, Estonia declared independence on 24 February 1918, and subsequently fought Soviet Russia and the German forces in the Estonian War of Liberation. In the ensuing peace treaty the Soviets recognized the Estonian Republic. During the following twenty years, the only time Estonia has been free since the thirteenth century, it raised its level of education to among the highest in Europe.

On 23 August 1939, Hitler and Stalin signed a non-aggression pact which contained a secret agreement to divide the Baltic States and Poland between them. After the outbreak of the Second World War, the Russians were soon back in Estonia.

The majority of the Estonians did not flee the Russians in 1940. They saw no reason to fear the Soviets. In 1941 the Germans pushed the Soviets back and it was the experiences of the Estonians during that one year of occupation (over 60,000 of them were killed or deported in one night) which led to panic when it was learned that they were coming back in 1944. The refugee exodus began. Those who had boats went to Sweden. Others had to rely on the retreating German convoys for a lift.

My mother was offered only one place in a boat to Sweden but there were three of us. I was aged seven. My grandmother was already sixty-five years old. My mother did the best she could because my father, who had told us he would join us, did not turn up.

We were among the last refugees, in September 1944. We had no boat and had missed the convoys. In a truck with several other people we drove to Saarema, one of the islands off the coast connected by a ferry. There we were picked up by a ship headed for Danzig.

From Danzig we went to Berlin, where my mother contacted the Dutch firm of Philips for whom she had worked before. They sent her to Porta Westphalica near Minden. We lived in the small village of Hausberge, in a Minister's attic, until the capitulation. Living in Hausberge I learned to speak German fluently in the village school.

After the capitulation in June 1945, Germany was divided into four Military Zones: French, Russian, English and American. Hausberge fell into the British zone. Refugee camps were established for all the now stateless refugees from the Baltic and from Eastern Europe, under the aegis of the United Nations Relief and Rehabilitation Administration – UNRRA in short.

We ended up in Meerbeck, near Hanover, in a DP camp especially for Estonians, Latvians and Lithuanians. And this is my story.

London
February 1978

Autumn to Winter 1947

1 The Secret Apple Mission

Chalk smelled like sweat. The classroom like a sauna. But it wasn't nearly as bad as Unki's socks, when he started undressing.

Nasal breathing. The scratching of pen nibs on paper. Teacher's pacing footsteps travelling between the desks, the blackboard, and the window. The glass was beaded with raindrops. The wind was shaking leaves off the autumn trees and pushing them along the road.

The teacher paused in her pacing briefly to raise her eyes to the sky. With hands clasped behind her back, she sighed a few times, deeply, then looked at her watch.

It was just eleven o'clock.

Suddenly, quite unexpectedly, the wings of a white butterfly touched down on the waxed floorboards. In sleepy forgetfulness, it lay still, waiting.

I turned to Rein and caught his desperate signals. I understood. But the teacher was already turning her heavy feet. Right shoe, then left shoe started back down the yellow wood, breaking stems and flowers in my mind, crushing all the ants and beetles in her path. Shoes like that belonged to giants, and I felt very small. There was nothing I could do. I sat tight and let the class breathe for me. The pens had stopped.

With her eyes to the ground, looking at her shoes, Mrs Vallas came upon the piece of paper with no apparent surprise. An expectant rustle swept the wooden benches, like wind blowing through a cornfield.

As in a dream, I watched her bend for the note. She began to open it, slowly, deliberately. I didn't have to wait long. A tight disturbance hovered around the teacher's mouth. She looked straight at me.

'An urgent telegram here for someone called Lotukata. Now I wonder who that can be.'

A tense silence filled the classroom.

'Very well,' she sighed. 'If the undermentioned is not here, we won't be able to forward this urgent message, will we? However, should she suddenly return, you might tell her to come and see me after class.'

Someone tittered. It sounded like Erika from the back bench. Mrs Vallas had put me in the front, to keep an eye on me. My ears were red hot all over. The teacher's eyes were on me, but I shut myself against her. I locked my teeth and stayed absolutely still, like a beetle when it is in danger. That way I knew she couldn't reach me, no matter how hard she tried. And I was right. A few moments later she was on her way again, the note tucked into her pocket.

Drats! I thought. I almost knew what the message was about, and it was important. Important enough to own up and stay after school.

All the camp roads were lined with apple trees. And this year I was an officer in the First House Gang, which meant taking part in the apple raid, though the German police had nailed warning signs on every tree: '*Verboten!*' It meant that anyone caught picking apples would be punished. Maybe even shot ... But after a year and a half in this camp, which was for displaced persons like us, who had nowhere to go, it wasn't a matter of 'life and death' anymore. Besides, the war was over. The shooting had stopped. This 'peacetime', as Memme, my grandmother had tried to explain, was now as real as American chewing gum. It was as real as Memme and Unki and my cat, called Cat.

'The filthy Fritzes,' I muttered under my breath, using Inge's favourite expression. We had watched those apples since blossom-time. I was chief taster, and Memme had wondered why I had diarrhoea all summer. That was just a part of it. Once or twice I had found myself with half a worm in my apple after having swallowed the first bite. So I knew where the other half had gone! But it was worth it, now that they were sweet and delicious and ready to be picked.

At long last the bell rang. I jumped up, grabbed my school bag and books, and would have been out the door if the teacher hadn't suddenly put a hand on my shoulder and pressed me back to my seat. 'Not so fast, young lady,' she said, smiling, and tapped her pocket.

Still smiling, Mrs Vallas pulled a chair close to the stove, opened a huge handbag, and took out her knitting. 'Write your message a hundred times,' she said pleasantly, and the needles started going click, click, click.

'Urgent. Meet in usual place after school. The Germans are putting guards on the trees tonight and picking the apples tomorrow. Stop.' At least I was grateful Rein hadn't used the usual code, which put 'stop' between each word. He must have been in a hurry. But so was I.

Mrs Vallas, unaware of the international crisis, had opened the stove door a bit and raised her legs to warm her panties. She began sucking out the fillings in her teeth, and once in a while she stopped knitting to scratch her head with the knitting needle. We all had head lice. Let them bite her! I wished they'd eat her up.

But again, after a year and a half of living 'normally' with people who went about their business just as we did, I knew she wouldn't hurt me. She might get angry and crack her knuckles at us, but she wouldn't beat me as Mr Koch used to beat me in the village school in Hausberge, where we lived before we came to the camp. 'Up the chimney with foreigners. *Verfluchter Ausländer!*' he called me. And he'd let the girls prod me with sharpened pencils. The boys had locked me in the toilets and shoved my clothes down the toilet bowl. None of the teachers had come to help me. On the way home from school I always had to pass a milliner's shop. The milliner's daughter Lisa had often lain in wait for me inside the doorway with her mother's hot hat iron.

I tried not to think about those wartimes anymore. In fact, I had almost forgotten them, but not quite – like during thunderstorms, when it all came back and Memme had to hold me as she used to hold me during air raids. In Berlin some big German boys had once carried me off to a backyard that had been hit in an earlier raid. They threw me down a bomb crater and started pelting me with rocks and broken bottles. An air raid saved me. The boys ran away. When the planes were already overhead, I could hear Memme calling me through shooting of the flak, the German anti-aircraft guns. She found me and dug me out. I never again dared play in that street, where I had been collecting spent cartridges from the gutter, to be made into whistles.

But the running had been the worst. Half asleep and not knowing which way to go in a strange city, I would hold on to Memme's hand, with her urging me on, as we stumbled across the piles of rubble that had been streets before, looking for the nearest air-raid shelter. In Berlin, the U-Bahn station, or subway, was sometimes the safest place to be. But if there was a crowd clogging the entrance, or there had been a cave-in or a direct hit on the shelter the night before, we had to lie down in the road. Memme always lay on top of me, telling me to keep my mouth open so that my eardrums wouldn't burst, and my eyes shut, so I wouldn't see the houses exploding. The explosions had haunted my sleep and given me nightmares, but I hadn't been really afraid when I was with Memme because she would always protect me. With Memme, I knew I was safe.

But another time I had been alone, running home from school after being locked in the toilet, and trying to get to Memme.

The sirens had stopped, and the planes were already overhead, flying low and strafing. I could hear the bullets bouncing off the cobblestones. And then I had been afraid.

All that was over now. Memme often said it was a miracle we were alive, but I thought it was a miracle just to sleep at night, without air raids, and to be in this camp for displaced persons, which to me was like a glass bubble. Inside the bubble, we were safe. We were still 'foreigners' and different, but we were Estonians, Latvians, and Lithuanians as well.

It had been Mimma, my mother, who had discovered the camp, just as she discovered everything and did everything for us. But now she had gone away again, ahead to England.

Mrs Vallas looked a bit like my mother. I tried to see Mimma again in my mind, as she had looked a year ago in the back of that big truck with a lot of other women. Memme said we would join Mimma 'eventually'. Just as my father was supposed to join us 'eventually' but we hadn't seen him since my seventh birthday. Memme, with a snort, said he was 'busy working in the theatre' and something about 'another woman'. He had been in a 'production' and got left behind. And I hated Mrs Vallas suddenly, for having the same hairdo as my mother and for sitting there and knitting her stupid jumper and scratching for lice and for not meaning anything more to me than being an Estonian. There she was, while all the people I had cared about, except Memme, who was my grandmother, and Unki, who was Memme's dead husband's youngest brother, had been left behind or had gone away – most of them sent to Verkuta in Siberia to the turf and salt mines. Or they had simply disappeared. But Unki had joined the French Foreign Legion, and had come back when he heard how things were with us. Mimma feared he had come back because his money was running out.

The stove was hot. Mrs Vallas opened the door some more and her legs began to turn red. My blanket suit was steaming from having been wet this morning and smelled a bit. It was made from one of Unki's grey army blankets, and it itched too.

I had lost count of the lines on the paper and all kinds of bad thoughts were going through my mind, when suddenly the weather changed. Even Mrs Vallas noticed it and raised her head. It was as if a big light bulb had been turned on in the sky. The rain clouds had parted. The raindrops on the windowpane began to sparkle like beads, as the sun streamed through the classroom window and onto my notebook.

It's a sign, I told myself happily. And along with the sun my whole mood changed. Thoughts about the past and other things were swept aside for another day or another thunderstorm. My punishment was almost over – well, nearly! – because the sun was out and the walk home to House Number Fifteen would be full of fresh rain puddles, and there would be earthworms popping out of the soil and crows dotting the fields waiting for them, like mourners in a village square. And I was happy because the Gang had accepted me at last and I belonged here.

Most of all I was happy because no matter what time I got home, Memme was waiting for me by the stove with something to eat, or with a supper that was always hot.

Sometimes Cat came to meet me halfway, to see if I was coming straight home or meeting the Gang. She, too, had been waiting for me and would even have come to school, only I didn't think Mrs Vallas would let her stay. And there were Inge and Väino and Leena, too. To think that only two years ago I didn't have a friend in the world except Memme!

I scribbled the last lines so fast my pen tore through the page. 'I've finished,' I shouted and thrust the crumpled sheaf at Mrs Vallas.

'Huh-huh!' was all she said. She didn't even look at it but chucked it straight into the fire. 'Well, go on,' she urged, as I stood staring at her – all that work for nothing! Grown-ups were really strange and never made any sense, I had already decided, but they never ceased to amaze me.

Free at last! I jumped out of the door and skipped the bright rain puddles, like mirrors against the sky and oceans afloat with oak leaves. Small ships were crossing the Baltic and steaming down the coast to Danzig. Such a ship had brought us from Estonia – Mimma, Memme and me. Three well aimed torpedoes sank the convoys with a splash. Tallinn was on fire. Rat-at-tat-tat! I got a direct hit. People were bobbing about in the water. A net was thrown overboard and they were hauled in like fish and dumped on deck. Old men, wounded, or women and children. Babies had been tied to their mother's backs but most were dead. Lots of dead, blown up like pigs' bladders.

Memme held me on her lap with difficulty because of the cork vests we were wearing. She was crying softly. But Mimma stood with the men, bareheaded. They were singing the Estonian national anthem. Mimma stood with the men 'because she has become the man of the family', Memme said often, 'for without her we would all be dead'.

'She doesn't understand,' said Mimma. But I did. I did! After I sunk the ships the water became still. Just puddles and oak leaves again.

I jumped another puddle and left the school yard, which was empty. Everybody had gone home. The swing in the meadow next to the school was also empty, with a huge puddle of water filling the hollow under the seat.

Summer was really over.

The sky was undecided – now sunny, now overcast, as the wind chased the clouds faster and faster into winter. When the sun did come out again, it showed how soggy and limp the grass had turned, and how the dead leaves that filled the gutters were becoming mouldy.

Let's face it, I thought, there won't be another summer till next year.

I passed the church and crossed the bridge between the Latvian and Lithuanian sectors. The little stream was slow moving and sluggish, with leaves and dead twigs floating on top. I added a dead twig of my own and watched it join the others on a course towards a rusty fence that marked the western boundary of the camp. Beyond it was German territory, and although there were no houses, just fields, I still looked at the fence a little anxiously.

Our house, Number Fifteen, was also on the German boundary, from the east side, and there was constant trouble.

Despite the sun, it was cold. The wind was playing a tune on my ear lobes. And it was saying, Come on, get moving, the Gang is waiting.

Then I remembered my hat. Memme was very strict about my wearing it and about keeping my jacket buttoned. She could always tell when I hadn't worn the hat. 'Your hair is cold,' she'd say, feeling it with her hand. 'Your ears are red.' And she would nod knowingly and start sorting her compresses.

I groped in my school bag, which was mostly full of horse-chestnuts and acorns, until I felt a velvety softness. There it was: my hat!

I took it out and ran it around my fingers. It really was a lovely hat. A droopy, doopy, loopy hat! A real Lotukata type of hat. And I was so proud of it.

When Memme first got it in an UNRRA shipment of winter clothes, I had hated it on sight. It was the middle of August, but just as Memme's summer starts in July, so her winter starts in August. She said I needed a winter hat.

When she came back from the camp warehouse, she looked mysteriously satisfied. She crooked a finger at me, with the other hand hidden behind her back, and as soon as I was close enough, she popped the hat over my head. In the dark, I shouted, 'Memme!'

'Never mind,' said Memme, lifting a corner so I could see her again. 'I'll take it in. All it needs is a few tucks here and there.' She went to look for a needle and thread.

'I won't wear it,' I told Memme, backing away. Nobody wore hats like that. It was of bright pink velvet with a big bow on one side, and had a green satin lining and knob on top. It didn't even look like a hat or a cap; it was more like a saucepan lid. It flopped and drooped on all sides.

'Tut, tut!' said Memme briskly, biting the cotton thread with her teeth. 'Think of the kind English or American lady who must have sent it to the United Nations Relief and Rehabilitation Association just so you could cover your head and keep your ears warm.'

'I just won't go out,' I said firmly.

But it was no use arguing with Memme over a matter of clothes. She simply put the hat back on my head and said we were expecting rain.

Never mind, I thought, I'll go about this my usual way. As soon as I was a safe distance from the house, I would stuff it into my trouser leg, as I did with the scarves and mittens I didn't want to wear.

But that day, too, I'd been in a hurry. The Gang was waiting by House Number One, and I was late already. We had planned to play 'police patrol' with our new scooters. Memme had just got me a new scooter in exchange for three packs of Camel cigarettes. The wheels were blue and silver and fairly purred after Unki had lubricated them with sardine oil.

I had been impatient to be away, but Memme still fussed with the hat, pulling it down farther and farther over my ears. Only then did she let me go, with the usual lecture: I must return at the first drop of rain. I was not to get my feet wet, and not to drink cold water. 'And don't run with your mouth open and swallow cold air,' she called after me from the window. Because she said the same things every time I left the house, I hardly heard them anymore.

The road to Number One was in full view of the window. I turned once and saw she was still there, watching me. I couldn't remove the hat just yet. That was bad enough! Then I saw that the Gang had already gathered, and they were fretting their scooter wheels impatiently on the hard asphalt. Rein, Vello, Tõnu, redhead Pügi, and Erika. They were all there.

Because of the hurry I was in, the hat drooped even lower. I could hardly see the ground. Nor did I have a free hand to push it back. Memme's eyes were still boring holes through the back of my head.

Muttering a couple of swear words under my breath, like Unki when he comes home drunk and can't locate the stairs, I pushed on.

I was not near enough yet to start braking, when Rein shouted, 'Hey, look, everybody, here comes Lotukata.' And then, 'Loppy Lotty, in her velvet potty!' The whole Gang ran out into the road, taking up the cry 'Lotukata! Lotukata!' (which means Kate with the funny hat.) They were jumping up and down around me, screaming and hooting like idiots. I was sure the whole camp could hear. And they did, because after that nobody called me Katrin any more, unless they were annoyed with me.

I was ready to tear the thing off my head and, if not jump on it (in consideration of Memme, who was still watching), stuff it into the nearest bush until it was time to go home. But Rein, the Gang leader, after circling around me for some time, decided it was not so bad, after all, except for the colour. Except for the colour, it could pass for an officer's beret. And he promoted me to 'officer' and Tõnu's aide. I had risen above the ranks of Erika and Vello, not to mention redhead Pügi, who wasn't even a corporal yet and was often caught sucking his thumb.

And now I wouldn't go anywhere without my Loppy. I carried my name with pride and just as proudly pulled the hat down as far as it would go.

I hated school. But going home was always fun. The camp was shaped like a triangle, and the schoolhouse was at the very top.

Our house, Number Fifteen, was down at the bottom, on the right-hand fork. There were no houses in the middle, just fields, and straight down the middle of the fields was a cart path. It was used mainly by the German farmers when they were allowed back into their former village to harvest their crops. Most of the time I never met anyone there but moles and rabbits. It was my secret road to and from school. I could lie down in the long grass or duck into the wheat fields or make footprints in the newly ploughed soil, according to the season. There was no one around to say No.

At Number Nine, I stopped for a minute, as usual, before jumping the ditch. We had lived there when we first arrived at the camp. I could just make out the little window behind the vines that had been 'ours'. But it wasn't ours anymore. Funny how a place was 'yours' one day. It was where you belonged and came home to, where you slept and ate, where you kept your things safe from others. But the next day it was just a house. You were not even allowed inside. Nothing we owned was 'ours'. We just used things and borrowed places, then gave them back. Like Memme borrowed Mrs Peterson's curling irons or a cup of sugar.

Only Memme was my own. My very own. Unki too. And Cat.

I jumped across the ditch and right away my clogs got stuck in the mud. I had forgotten. The clogs, too, were UNRRA-issue camp clogs, with wooden soles and canvas uppers. The wood wasn't polished, and everything stuck to it. My feet were full of blisters. Unki had promised to wind rags around my feet first thing in the morning, but he often forgot or was hung over. School started so early, at half past seven. 'I'll do it tonight,' he would promise for sure, so I could sleep in them. But he usually stayed at the brewery till late. Memme said she could knit me some socks from an old cardigan she was unravelling. I said I didn't want socks, I wanted rags like Unki's. And I wanted Unki to wind them for me, as the soldiers did in the Foreign Legion.

I found the field path really bleak. The wind blew even stronger out in the open. It whipped up the mouldy grass and chased stubble and old potato stalks from one ditch to another. The wheat and rye had been harvested weeks before, and now the farmers were into the last of the beets, potatoes, and turnips. A few German carts stood among the crows while the farmer and his wife bent over their harvest, or what there was left of it. They couldn't do it fast enough, being only allowed into the camp during daylight. They killed a British soldier and so their farms were taken over to make the camp, but they couldn't take their fields or crops with them. It made them very angry, and although they were allowed to do their own harvesting this way, there were only a few of them and so many of us.

At night the fields were crowded with refugees bumping into each other in the dark with bags and sacks and bowls and buckets.

It started usually around midnight. I woke up, too, because of a great whispering going on in the hall and on the stairs: people creeping around with lighted candles, sacks, and baskets. Last night I had followed Unki down the stairs and hidden behind the well to watch. The field between us and the mill opposite was full of shadows, bending and digging with bare hands for turnips and potatoes, all illuminated for a moment by a shift in the clouds. I had wanted to go too, but Memme, standing with a sack in the shadow of the drainpipe, had ordered me back to bed.

But we figured that if the grown-ups could ignore the '*Verboten*' signs, so could we. And we meant to get those apples. Without apples, winter would not be the same. Memme dried them, cooked them, or cut them up raw as medicine when I got the fevers.

I was almost home.

A quick supper and I'd be off. House Number Sixteen looked quiet, but I hesitated before going through the gate. They had a mean-tempered goose there that didn't like me. As soon as it saw me it always came running with its neck arched, hissing and snapping its beak. But there was no sign of the goose. It was locked up.

I crossed the yard and ran across the road to Number Fifteen, which was home. It was a good feeling to come home. The huge carriage entrance to the farmhouse had a hard-packed dirt floor, like all the other German farmhouses. This was where the farmer usually kept his cart and harness. The rooms all faced the hall. Stairs led to the rooms on the second-floor landing. Our room was the last on the right, next to the attic.

Although all the houses were alike, none of the others smelled like ours – or sounded like ours. From the door I could already hear Mrs Peterson's voice shouting over sizzling onions and the other women's voices shrill and excited in the communal kitchen as they quarrelled and searched for missing pots and pans and got their dinners ready. There was only one kitchen, and only those who didn't have stoves of their own used it. We had our own pots and pans and our own stove. I couldn't get over the wonder of it. And Unki was so proud too. He had found it and installed it all by himself.

I breathed in the burning fat and the smell of pigs in the pigsty. The women's voices eased my mind every time. Sometimes I just stopped and listened or came home afraid I wouldn't hear them. I was still afraid I would find the house empty and cold one day, or find a cold stove without any supper on it – or no stove at all, just a crust of bread in a cold, damp cellar, as it used to be.

I hoped we would stay here a while longer. Not forever, mind you, but until Christmas, at least. Then we could have a tree and candles, cake and biscuits baked in old tin cans, like last year. Memme stacked tin lids on top of one another on the stove, three for bread, four for cakes, and balanced a tightly sealed biscuit tin on top with a large coffee tin, or whatever was handy, of batter inside it. Memme baked the best things in the camp and no one knew how she did it. When the other women asked her about it, she said it was nothing, when in fact it took all day. Sometimes the stack fell over, or the labels on the old tins caught fire and burned through, and she had to start over again. If the cakes tasted of sauerkraut or sardines, depending on the tin she was using, that too was a part of it.

The thoughts of food and cooking and the friendly kitchen sounds made me feel warm and loved, the way I felt when I was being held close, and it gave me such a sense of boldness that I changed my mind and tiptoed back into the yard. Around the corner of the house was the well and, next to it, a pear tree. One branch grew at right angles exactly level with the attic window.

Making sure no one had spotted me, I jumped from the well cover to the lowest branch, hung there a second, pulled my feet up, and climbed on quickly. The window was already wedged open with a stick. In no time at all, I was inside the attic, directly over the kitchen, where Mrs Peterson had had to throw her burning pan into the sink, having forgotten it again. It usually happened when she got carried away in a conversation or started tasting Mrs Mölder's potato soup or carrot pudding.

Stepping across the attic over the hall was tricky. The floor boards had big spaces between them and any straw that fell through landed in the hall, right outside the house superintendent's door. I had been warned a hundred times to stay out of the attic.

The ladder was up and the door to the landing was shut. I listened carefully before I opened it and jumped down onto the landing. Then I stepped into our room, trying to look innocent.

Memme was stirring the soup kettle on the wood-burning stove. I threw my school bag on the bed. 'What's for dinner?' I asked brightly.

'Bread soup,' said Unki, climbing doubled-up out of his little chamber.

Again!

'Did you come by the front door?' asked Memme.

'How else?'

Unki sat on the bench next to me and dug me with his elbow. Memme gave me a knowing nod but turned back to the soup.

'Has the food truck been around yet?'

'Not yet,' Unki answered. He opened his penknife and went to work. He was carving Memme a wooden spoon for Christmas so she could throw away the stick she used to stir with. I watched the penknife. How I wished it were mine. It had three blades and a corkscrew as well as a thing to pick your teeth with.

'Eat your soup,' said Memme, putting the full plate down carefully. When it was very full, I was allowed to sip over the side a little but not to slurp.

I ate as quickly as I could. Usually on Thursdays, I met the food truck and hung on to the back. But today there were more important things to attend to.

Finished! I jumped up, but Memme pulled me back. 'What about your homework?'

Gosh! Another delay and I'd miss the whole thing!

Memme looked at me sternly.

'There's time enough,' I told her.

'There is never time enough,' answered Memme in her typically mysterious way. She removed the plates. Unki gathered his shavings to one corner and I didn't have any choice.

Soon Memme had finished by the stove. She took up her pencil and pad and sat on the bed opposite me, so she could sketch me while I worked.

For a moment I thought I might tell Unki about the apple picking and maybe get some 'strategy', but then I changed my mind. Even Unki had his limits. Today's yes might well be tomorrow's no. And Memme wouldn't like it.

Unki's knife went *siuh, sauh* as it sliced down the spoon handle. Shavings flew. My pen scratched frantically. I was always late! Memme's pencil ran smoothly across her pad. Another time I might have stayed home to draw with her or ask to do her hair in a hundred plaits. She had long grey hair, so long she could sit on it, and I loved to give her funny styles. One time I had plaited ten braids all around her head, when Mrs Ott, from the room next to ours, came to borrow some flour. Memme was beside herself trying to undo her hair. Finally she threw a towel around her head. She said she had just washed her hair. But she didn't know that one plait was hanging down her ear, outside the towel. Mrs Ott was looking at it and didn't know what to make of it all.

When we were together like this, homework usually went fast. Memme always ate with me. 'Two pigs eat better than one,' she'd say.

The air above the stove was blue and acrid. The soup kettle bubbled softly, awaiting renewed appetites. Sparks of resin crackled and hissed in the fire, and sometimes a few sparks escaped the badly fitted door. The floor around the stove was charred and pitted. Unki had promised to nail some tin down under it, 'one of these days'.

If Unki wasn't carving a spoon he would be doing something else or taking a nap with the trapdoor open. Unki lived in a secret chamber off our room. We had discovered the chamber by accident. The door was so well concealed, he himself had difficulty finding it late at night with a noseful. And when Unki wasn't home, we kept the table in front of the door. No one knew about it. It was our secret, and we kept things in there that we were not supposed to have, like apples and the other vegetables and all the stuff under Unki's bed – mostly empty bottles. Muki had lived there too. Poor sad rabbit!

'Count on your fingers,' suggested Memme from the bed. She had seen that I was stuck with my arithmetic. 'That's what they're for.'

'I can't!' I almost cried in frustration. The clock had stopped again, but I knew it was nearly time. The others would have finished eating hours ago and were probably already getting their orders.

And just then I heard a loud snort and an 'Aaah'. It sounded like someone being strangled. But it was only Mrs Angoroff starting her throat-clearing exercises, which she did every day before sundown, through her open window. It was a Russian custom, like Unki blowing his nose with the side of his thumb.

Memme put down her pad and held her pencil at eye level for perspective. She saw the plight I was in. It was hopeless!

Memme put the pencil away and came to the table. The safety pins rattled noisily against her bosom. Memme always wore safety pins fastened to her front, 'in case', and they got caught on things.

She sat down heavily. Her breathing was short and laboured. She had trouble with asthma and sometimes got attacks. But she also had a habit of puffing and panting for no reason at all. I asked her, 'Why are you puffing?' Memme laughed and said she had inherited it from her father. He had puffed and panted for no reason at all.

We looked at the sum together, and Memme shook her head. I'd been only practising with the pen, without any ink on it, I explained, regarding the ink spots. I couldn't imagine how they happened.

Memme read the problem. 'Better show it to Paul.'

'Oh, no,' said Unki. 'Not me. I had enough of that in my time.'

'If one man travels three miles in two hours . . .' Memme read aloud over her glasses and smiled. 'Without calling in at the brewery, he might get home for supper!'

The question was, 'If one man travels three miles in two hours, how long would it take for two men travelling together to cover the same distance at the same pace?'

'If it took your Uncle Paul two hours to get home from

Stadthagen on his own, how long would it take if the two of you had gone together?'

I thought about that, and no mention of the brewery, which meant we would come home together. 'It would take the same time.'

'Justament!' said Memme happily. Justament is one of Memme's own words. It means that-is-just-what-I-meant.

The rest was easy. I don't know what I'd do without Memme!

I sneaked out so that Inge or Väino would not see me. Inge wanted to join the Gang too. She was only five – but a good strong five, I had to admit, reluctantly.

When I finally arrived at the brewery, Rein, with chin forward, and hands behind his back, was pacing up and down the mound of hops.

'You're late!' he barked.

'I know – the teacher, my shoes, homework ...'

Rein, Tõnu, Vello, Erika, and redhead Pügi looked at me sternly. I had forgotten. An officer does not make excuses.

Rein swept us into a circle around the mound. We squatted down to await orders.

'We're moving in right away,' said Rein importantly. 'It will be dark in half an hour. We must get there before the guards arrive. First of all ...' He drew a map of the road in the hardened mud. 'The trees are here and here, between Number One and Number Fifteen. These are the most difficult, in the open and in full view of the German farm.'

He let this sink in a moment. Pügi thought he heard his mother calling him but Rein cut him short.

'If the police should come, the two underneath the tree must start running, to distract attention. Then, while they are being chased, those up the tree can climb down and escape.'

'But suppose the police don't chase the first two at all but stay right there?' I asked.

Rein threw me a threatening look. I had forgotten again. A soldier does not challenge the leader but keeps his mouth shut.

We were ready to go. I pulled my hat down low over my eyes, crushed the apple sack to my fast-beating heart, and remembered it was an honour to be trusted with the sack in the first place.

We moved out in single file, crouching low along the ditch. The ditch was half full of water. The edges of my blanket trousers were soon heavy with mud. And it was cold. The sky was clearing and the moon had a halo around it. It was going to be full again tonight. It would!

We reached the first tree, and my teeth were chattering, whether from fear or from cold, I didn't know.

The climbing part should have been easy. It was an old tree. Rein and Tõnu stayed below to guard us and catch the apples. But there were too many of us, all going up at once. It was hard to find a footing without standing on someone's head or hand. It was impossible to be quiet. Redhead Pügi was the worst. Now he was up, he was stuck, said he couldn't go any farther. He was blocking the way for Erika, and said she was pushing him.

'Shut up!' shouted Rein from below. Tõnu also got nervous and started shushing. So we shushed each other, though Pügi was still in the way.

But there were plenty of apples on the lower branches. We set to work. A few minutes later, I thought I heard again what I had heard before.

Distant barking and voices on the German farm.

'It's milking time,' said Rein. 'But hurry!'

I thought milking time was in the morning.

The apples were soon raining down and it was fun. I threw a few at Tõnu and he jumped aside. Then I threw another few a bit farther down the ditch, as far as I could. I knew I would get my share, but it would hardly be worth it. So I thought I would salt a few and come back for them later.

With all the throwing and shouting, I clean forgot about the dogs, till suddenly they seemed to be much closer! And there was a creaking and rattling sound. I took a quick look up the road, and my heart skipped a beat. A shadowy column of people was bearing down on us along the road. They had a farm cart with them. The sound of the wheels was like a terrifying, hollow moaning, cutting across the quiet camp.

Then I saw Rein and Tõnu in the distance, legging it over the potato field.

All panic broke loose at the top of the apple tree. Escape was impossible. While it had been too crowded to climb up, it was now even harder to get down. I stepped on Erika's head, and she screamed, throwing redhead Pügi off balance. He screamed too and fell off into the ditch.

The police! And the German farmers.

'*Rrrrrausss!*' shouted the policeman furiously, and tugged at my leg. Pügi was still screaming and Erika was crying. She had torn her shirt.

The policeman shook us by the shoulders, shouting and threatening to shoot us. But of course they didn't. They didn't even chase us, as we ran for our lives.

Next day I asked Rein why he and Tõnu had run off so early. He explained that, in war, generals always retreat first or stay at a safe distance. Who ever heard of a general getting caught?

2 The Raid

It was raining again, as it did so often now. And I got so wet going to school and back that I had to spend the rest of the day standing by the window in my underclothes, while my blanket suit was drying by the stove.

There was nothing to do except race raindrops down the window glass. It was some weeks after the apple raid. We had plenty of apples, but I was already tired of coring and paring them and threading them on strings to be hung in Unki's chamber to dry. That was what Memme was doing.

Unki was lying on his bed reading a book with a torn cover. Memme had made him tear it off and throw it in the fire, but not before I caught a glimpse of a bare bottom and black suspenders.

What a day, I thought, with nothing to do but watch a line of jeeps coming down the road from Stadthagen. There must have been a hundred of them.

'Look at all those jeeps, Unki,' I called in the way of conversation.

'Uh-huh,' said Unki, without looking up from his book.

'They've stopped by Number One house, and there's soldiers with rifles and –'

'Soldiers!' Unki jumped from his bed as though someone had pricked his behind. 'Police!' he shouted, and dashed out the door. 'Quick, give the word. Tell them it's a raid.'

'Here,' shouted Memme. She threw a summer dress at me. 'Run over to Sixteen and pass the word. Go as fast as you can.'

And already she was throwing the apple cores and apples and the rest of it into Unki's chamber.

As I ran down the stairs, all the doors were open. People were running in all directions, shouting 'Raid!' and making for the pigsty. A knife flashed. The Angoroffs' pig, I thought, but I knew it was urgent. I cursed my shoes and didn't even notice the rain. In the hall of Number Sixteen, I shouted for Linda's father, but they already knew. Their door was open, and I could see Linda sitting on her bed, clutching her pet piglet. Besides that they had two more pigs and that goose. And here, too, everybody was running around the hall in a panic.

Linda's father grabbed my shoulder and pushed me outside again. 'Pass the word in the village. And hurry!'

As I crossed the yard I noticed that the jeeps were still standing at Number One. I could beat them if it weren't for these shoes. I ploughed on.

But next time I turned and looked back, I saw that the column had divided and the soldiers were well on their way. Some had turned up our fork and the others were heading at top speed towards the village and were already parallel with me.

It was useless to go on.

I wondered where Unki had got to and then started worrying about Memme. I hurried back to the house as fast as I could. The police were already there, with guns. There were two types of police, German police and Military Police, and they had already started searching the downstairs rooms.

I burst into our room and stopped short in amazement. Was this our room? I stood there with my mouth open but there was Memme sitting calmly at the table reading her book 'Meditations' as if she had been sitting there all day. All the furniture had been moved. Half our bundles were missing, and the table was placed so that it completely blocked the chamber door, with Memme sitting right up against the entrance. Unki was nowhere to be seen.

'Memme . . .' I started, but Memme put a shushing finger to her lips. She handed me a pack of boiled sweets that were as big as robin's eggs.

'Sit at the window and keep your mouth shut. Those should help, and if anybody asks you a question, you don't know!' she whispered.

I nodded, popped a sweet into my mouth, and from then on couldn't have talked if I wanted to.

Memme had barely finished whispering when there was a loud rap on the door, and it was flung open even before Memme could say 'Come in'. Which she did slowly and calmly, one finger still on her page. 'Yes?' she asked, surprised, and quite a bit annoyed at all this rudeness.

Two Military Policemen stood at the door, with a German Policeman behind them and with the superintendent hovering in the background wringing his hands. 'This is an outrage!' he kept repeating.

I was glad my mouth was crammed full of sweets because I recognized the German policeman from the apple raid, and also because I had known words to escape from my mouth all by themselves. This way they couldn't.

The two MPs stepped into the centre of the room and looked around.

'*Machen Sie alles auf!*' the German policeman barked at Memme. He was telling her to open everything.

Memme began untying our bundles, spreading their contents on the bed.

The two MPs started searching the room. They stuck bayonets into the mattresses and under the beds, and one of them even looked into the stove.

It was all very exciting, but scary too. An argument had started between Memme and the German policeman. He said she had stolen that silver. Memme said she had not. Memme's German was very good and she was very indignant. She showed him the monograms on the handles of the spoons. 'That was a part of my trousseau,' she told him, waving a spoon at him. 'And the sugar tongs belonged to my grandmother. The tea strainer was given to me by a German pastor friend of my father's before the war. His son became a high-ranking official in the German army, though God knows what has happened to him now.' Memme's voice got quite chatty, and the policeman became a bit embarrassed.

'I'm only doing my duty, ma'am! We have definite information that the refugees are stealing food from the German farmers and keeping animals, also stolen, against regulations. The search is under the authority of the occupying army.'

He began tapping the walls and floorboards.

'But, Captain,' said Memme, promoting him in rank. 'Who would do such a thing? Stealing food and keeping animals! Certainly not the Estonians,' said Memme, though she said she had heard that people exchanged things for cigarettes on the black market. And she admitted that she herself had had to do so a few times to get a few extras for the child. Meaning me. But as for keeping animals or stealing . . .

The policeman agreed these were hard times for everybody. He complimented Memme on her German and got quite friendly. 'This pastor,' he asked, 'his name didn't happen to be Schulzbauer, did it, from Linz?'

I stuck to my chair like a limpet to a rock. One of the MPs was over by the table, tracing the pattern of the wallpaper with his finger and looking puzzled.

Any moment now . . . I felt my body straining forward, as his finger moved closer and closer to the secret door. The suspense was so awful and the anxiety so great that I forgot to hold on to my sweets. There was a sudden swoosh and clatter as the bag fell from my hand and the contents of boiled sweets went shooting in all directions.

For a second everybody was startled. The policemen clutched

their rifles at the ready. And then they all started laughing. The man at the wallpaper lost his pattern and went to retrieve a sweet that had rolled under the table. The others started picking up sweets too and popped them in their mouth, but found they could only manage one at a time.

'Let's go,' said one of the MPs. He apologized to Memme for the 'inconvenience'. The German policeman clicked his heels in a smart salute, and they all left. We heard them knocking next door.

Memme and I were alone again. But Memme kept a finger on her lips until we heard the heavy boots going down the stairs. Only then did she let me off my chair to collect the rest of my sweets, while she started redoing her bundles.

A sudden shout in the hall. Angry voices in Estonian and German. I wanted to take a look. Memme said, 'No!'

We waited some more.

A long time later, when the jeeps were back on the road to Stadthagen again, I saw Memme smile. She hugged me, and together we pushed the table away from the wall. Unki stepped out of his chamber, laughing all over his gold teeth. He threw me up to the ceiling and said he was so proud of me. No one else would have thought of throwing the bag of sweets down as I did. The reason Unki had to hide was because most men were supposed to be in the army. But on his way back from Indo China, Unki had sold his French passport for a bottle and he had no papers, yet.

'Really?' I asked.

'What a brave girl you are,' he told me again and again. Memme said so too.

I didn't remember throwing the bag of sweets down on purpose, but on the other hand, I could have done so.

I thought I was a real hero, until I heard what Mari Kont had done. She was in my class at school. The whole camp was talking about her the next day. She had gathered together all the pigs at

House Number Eight and driven them into a nearby wood. The police had seen her and stopped her. They asked her what she was doing, but she turned right around and told them in German that she was the new herdsgirl for the German farm across the field and had brought the pigs in from the rain. Those were German pigs, she said, and she knew nothing about the camp except that her master had told her to keep out of it.

Every one of those pigs was saved!

'Never mind,' said Unki.

Still, it could have been me. My German was as good as Mari's, and there was a wood close by and everything. I knew I could have done better. I would have saved all the animals in the whole camp, at least a hundred of them.

The police found the Petersons' pig in Mrs Peterson's bed, tucked under the covers. It was taken away.

The Mölders hurriedly killed theirs and hung it in the well. The Angoroffs hid the carcass of theirs in the bushes across the road. Now everybody was busy salting pork and grumbling because they had been fattening the pigs for Christmas.

Rein told me his father had killed their pig, dressed it up in his mother's hat and coat, and sat it on the toilet. 'Excuse me, ma'am!' the policeman had apologized and immediately closed the door again. Tõnu argued that it was their pig, not Rein's. And at least ten others had done the same thing. I didn't know whom to believe!

Unki was slapping his thighs as he told us how Linda's father had given their three piglets a bottle of vodka to share and his wife had taken them dead drunk up into the attic and hidden them in the straw. But the piglets had snored so loud that she had been scared stiff they would be heard.

They had to kill the goose. I was glad of that – till I heard they were going to get a new one.

But it wasn't all fun and heroes, as I later found out at school.

The Latvians had had plenty of time to hide their things. By the time the police had gotten to their part of the camp, the people had all come out to meet them. They told the police to search at will, they had nothing to hide. They had not laid eyes on a pig for years.

The police had searched and found nothing until suddenly this little girl had stepped out of the bushes, holding her pet piglet in her arms. It was like a kitten to her, like Linda's piglet Notsu. It had a red ribbon around its neck, and when she heard the policemen talking about pigs, she had wanted to show them hers.

Instead of stroking and petting it, the policeman had grabbed it away from her by force. Her parents had protested and pleaded that it was only a pet and the little girl had refused to part with it. In the end the policeman had had to slap her to push her away. And they had killed the piglet right there before her eyes.

When I heard that, I realized I had forgotten Berlin and Hausberge a little too quickly, and had put a bit too much trust into this 'peacetime', which had solved hardly anything at all. I was glad Muki was dead now, or they would have killed him too.

3 Another Time, Another Place

Not long after that, I met Cat.

It was most unfortunate. The last thing I needed was another pet. I had vowed I would never get involved with another pet as long as I lived. I resolved to harden my heart at the very beginning. No more heartaches.

I called her Cat. I warned her I wouldn't love her. I couldn't love her. Loving meant being miserable, always waiting, wanting, or being left behind. It meant being hurt, getting into misunderstandings.

'Go away, Cat,' I said. 'Your kind is nothing but trouble.' I ignored her.

I didn't even ask her to follow me. She came all by herself. 'You have all those fields to play in,' I told her. 'Besides, we're not allowed animals. I already have a rabbit. If the superintendent sees you, he'll put you in a bag and throw you in the canal.' There was a canal about two miles from the village.

But did she care? 'Dumb cat,' I said. She was German, couldn't understand Estonian anyway. Big fat thing with black and white markings, she just rubbed herself against my legs and purred. I couldn't help stroking her, she was so soft and silky.

'I'll have to ask Memme first.'

I sat on the edge of the well and dragged her up to my lap. She didn't even mind being dragged by the forelegs. Mother said it makes them sick. But not this cat. This cat didn't mind anything. She started kneading my lap, closed her eyes, and purred softly.

'You know I'd like to keep you, but I can't. You must go

home,' I pleaded desperately, my fingers deep in the white fur.

'You'll have to go,' I repeated firmly, and took her to Memme.

Memme hardly looked up. 'No.'

'But, Memme . . .'

'I said no, no, no, no!'

'She could lick out the sardine cans.'

'No. Besides, she's a female,' said Memme, taking a closer look. 'That means more trouble.'

But Memme was still my Memme! Half an hour later, Cat was lapping condensed milk beside the stove.

'But be sure the superintendent doesn't see her,' warned Memme over and over again.

I repeated this to Cat, and she nodded. Then I put my cheek against her soft one. 'Hello, Cat,' I said in Estonian, as she had to learn it sometime. 'You're one of the family now, but please, please don't run off.' And I suggested she go and live in the attic. It was the safest place. Also, she would have to catch her own food. Memme said we didn't have enough.

Cat said it was all right. She agreed to everything.

'She has an old soul,' said Memme. That explained it, of course.

One dry Sunday between a lot of wet ones, Unki reached for his greatcoat, took his knapsack off the peg, and said, 'Come on, Lotukata!'

Cat came too. I had to wake her from a nap, but like the good soldier she was, she didn't complain. As she was under strict orders not to love me, we talked very formally. I had made it clear there was to be no more 'loving and leaving' in this camp. Still, I couldn't resist hugging her soft fat body once in a while.

Unki said, 'Let's go mushrooming together.' The woods around the camp were full of wild mushrooms. Unki had taught me how to smell the difference between a mushroom and a toadstool. 'If they smell sweet,' he said, 'they are good.' I understood, but I liked the pretty red ones best. So I picked mine and he picked his.

It was a lovely day for a change. The sun was shining golden, like Unki's teeth. The birds were hopping about in the bushes teasing Cat, who nearly went mad trying to catch them all. With Unki there were few no-nos. He didn't say do this or do that. Sometimes he got his feet wet too, and we both dried off together, promising each other not to tell Memme.

Unki helped me climb a tree, and then we had refreshments.

Memme had packed some rye bread in a napkin. Cat and I drank from a stream while Unki drank from his flask. I asked him to give me a little sip from his flask too, just a sip. He did. It tasted awful, and I spat it right out. It was the same stuff that Memme put on my cuts as a disinfectant. I couldn't imagine how Unki could drink it, but I guess he could, being a man. He said you could drink it if you were a man. 'If you're a lady and you drink it, it looks bad.' Then he jammed the cork back into the flask.

Cat discovered an ant hill. We put some bread crumbs near it and watched the workers try to lift them. Unki said ants have the biggest brains in relation to their bodies and they always know what they are doing. He said they would never pick poison mushrooms for the fun of it, because they would know it was dangerous.

Unki's knapsack was full, but it was still early. He said it was time to do his 'rounds'. Unki had never taken me before, but he did them often, usually on Sundays.

We reached the edge of the forest. A German village lay below us, in a valley. Chimneys smoked. A church bell was ringing. I wondered why the camp church bell never rang. I had not yet been to church, but Memme had told me about them, and about how you prayed to Jesus kneeling down on a wooden board instead of just anywhere or beside my bed, as Memme did when

I was sick. Memme said it didn't matter where you prayed as long as 'the spirit moves you'. Like Daniel, who prayed in the lion's den.

I didn't want to go into the German village. From where we stood it looked like Hausberge. Cat said she didn't want to go either, so I cradled Cat in my arms and told Unki we would wait for him. We could sit on a log and rest, and he could pick us up on the way back.

Unki wouldn't hear of it.

I stayed a little behind him, just in case, and held Cat, whose fur was rising. Fierce dogs started barking as soon as we approached the first gate, and it was hard to hold Cat at all.

But Unki barely lifted the latch before the farmhouse door opened and the Frau came out, like a boat in full sail, all aprons and skirts. She was wearing the local folk costume that all the women wore, even in the fields. On weekdays it was green and black, and on Sundays it was red and black. There was a little frilly cap perched on the top of her head and masses of lace around her neck and cuffs.

She was a young woman with rosy cheeks and untidy hair, and Unki seemed to know her well. She seemed to have been waiting for him. Unki's mouthful of gold teeth set her all giggling and repinning her hair, as she led us into the kitchen.

And what a kitchen! With a rush of tears I stared at the huge iron range in one corner and the kitchen table under the window, at a pot boiling and the steam on the windowpane.

Unki and the Frau seemed to have forgotten me as a sort of game began. Unki wanted to chase her around the table, but she pushed him away, with an 'Oih' and an 'Aih' and a '*Lass mal, das Kind sieht doch!*' Not in front of the child! But all the time she was pushing him away, she was really getting closer to him. Once she bit Unki's earlobe as she reached across him to get some plates out of a cupboard. And Unki kept his arm around her waist the whole time she laid out a platter of ham and bread ‘for the dear child’, filled a pitcher with milk, and placed it all before me. Then with a sudden ‘Uih,’ as Unki pinched her quite hard, she let him steer her off to another room ‘to fix her bedroom lamp’, Unki told me from the doorway.

As soon as they had closed the door between us I looked around the kitchen again, but I dared not eat. In all the places we have ever stayed at, in attics or cellars, we had never been allowed inside the landlady’s part of the house. I had never been inside a German kitchen before, and no German woman had ever called me ‘dear child’.

But worse still, I had forgotten that all the kitchens in the world were the same. I had forgotten that they all had big tables and little tables that could be polished and covered by clean lace tablecloths, and that there could be a vase of autumn marigolds in the centre, next to a plate of ham. There was a grandfather clock ticking calmly in a corner – ‘Pendulously,’ Memme always used to say in the old times, when she let me pull down the weights once in a while.

But it was the range I remembered most. I couldn’t move in my chair for remembering. Our stove had been built into the wall too, and you could set six pots on it. One of them was always boiling and misting up the windows – cooking sauerkraut or heating water for my bath or boiling the bristles off a side of bacon.

And there had been just such a ledge underneath it, where a cat could sleep all day on the warm bricks, where Tätä, Memme’s sister, had let the bread rise and the milk sour. Taat and Tätä and Tondu, my cat, whom I had loved and lost . . .

The sun streaked through the misty window onto the gay flowers and the polished tables and the little linen tablecloths. The grandfather clock went boom! boom! But Tätä wasn’t coming back from the well. And my father wasn’t coming home from the theatre and Tondu wasn’t going to scratch at the door to be let in. All was silent in the German kitchen.

I felt so tired suddenly that I put my head down. I didn’t want to see the polished pots and pans anymore, when all Memme had was the old coffee tins and lard containers that I had been so proud of. And I cried because the marigolds were in a real vase instead of a jam jar.

There was a giggle in the bedroom. I pushed Cat angrily off my lap.

Life was all nonsense, like having a dream and waking up, or being awake but not realizing that you are in fact dreaming and that all life might be a dream. Unki and Memme had discussed that one day over dinner.

As the bedroom lamp was obviously not fixed yet (Unki always fixed things in the bedroom for these women), I decided to give Cat a little treat. I put the whole platter of ham on the floor and I let Cat make a pig of herself all over the nice Frau's polished kitchen tiles. I guessed the husband was dead or in Siberia, like most husbands. I didn't touch the milk or the bread. Instead I did something else that was naughty. I demolished the marigolds one by one and left the petals scattered on the tablecloth, dying in the sunlight.

At the gate, before we left, the lady gave Unki an apronful of fresh eggs, still warm and covered with chicken dirt.

At the next farm, we only stayed long enough for the lady to wrap a piece of bacon into a towel. And at the third place, Unki received 'a little pot of butter'. At every farmhouse the lady saw us to the gate, and it was always with the same parting promise. 'Ten pounds of coffee beans from Brazil!' said Unki. 'I won't forget.'

When we were finally through and on the way home again, our pockets were bulging and Unki's knapsack wouldn't close. I asked him, 'Where are you going to get ten pounds of coffee? Where is Brazil?' But Unki only laughed and pinched my cheek.

'*Mit Speck fängt man Mäuse,*' he whispered into my ear, and winked. With a little bait, you were sure to catch a mouse!

*

It was hard for me to get up for school in the morning when it was still dark. All the best parts of autumn were over, the trees were bare, and the bushes were ragged thickets of dead twigs.

When it was wet and dark and cold, I wanted to cuddle back in the warm straw mattress. When I heard the wind whistling around the house and the rain beating on the window, I pulled the blanket over my head and stopped being.

Memme awakened me as gently as she could. She knew how I felt about getting up for school on such a morning. She didn't feel too good herself. Being bad risers ran in our family.

Memme always got up first to light the stove. If Unki had forgotten to bring in the wood, it was wet and spat and hissed from being in the rain all night. It was cross and grumpy as any bear would have been, I reminded Memme. And I reminded her that all the squirrels and hedgehogs were still sleeping and that dark was for night and light for day. She told me so herself when it was bedtime. No electric bulb was going to change it, shaded or not by Memme's old fringed shawl.

By the time the wood was burning and the flour gruel was bubbling in the pot, I had managed to sit up. Memme handed me a cup of warm powdered milk, diluted with water. She never said 'Get up' but 'It is time'. By now the words had lost their terrifying wartime meaning.

Memme washed my face with a rag dipped in the water bucket or, if Unki had forgotten to fill it, with water from the coffeepot. She dressed me and braided my hair, while I kept my eyes shut, partly because of the smoke from the wet logs – it filled the room to the ceiling – and partly because I was trying to finish a dream.

Supporting my chin above the plate, I wished some magic force would carry me to school, just as I wished it would take me to the toilet during the night, down the stairs, through the cold hall and pigsty, without my having to wake up.

Väino, who lived downstairs, walked to school with me, when his mother remembered to get him ready. Most times she didn't.

At Sixteen I waited for 'poor chest', actually Linda, but as her mother never talked about anything but 'Linda's poor chest', I called her that in my mind. Linda's mother opened the window and shouted down that Linda wasn't coming. 'It's her poor chest!' We said it together, I under my breath, as I hid a smile.

Linda's mother wagged a warning finger at me and slammed the window shut. She must have heard me.

Leena was ready and waiting. Her *babushka* (which meant 'grandmother' in Russian) was there too and gave us each an apple and a kiss. She made friendly noises I could understand. Babushka could speak only Russian, and saw us through the gate. I liked her. She was another version of Memme, except that she wore a scarf in public. Memme never wore a scarf in public. She only wore a scarf to bed, or when she was cooking and perspiring and her 'pores were open'. Sometimes she wore a towel around her head and shoulders for the same reason.

Leena and I didn't talk much. I had worked hard to be her best friend. I had even learned some Russian so I could speak to her, but she rarely said more than yes or no. The other kids still teased her about being Russian. I felt guilty about her because I'd had a hand in it too. I wanted to be her friend, but I also wanted to be popular with the others.

At school we were learning English. Mimma had sent me lots of English books that I hoped to read one day, but there were so many hundreds of words in them that it looked hopeless.

As soon as the teacher said, 'Open your books at page nine,' I thought, Here we go again, and slipped away for my private game of 'imagination'. I closed my eyes and let myself be carried off on a picture in my mind to another time and another place. While the class was intoning 'My name is John', I hurried back to Haapsalu, to our little house on the lagoon where I had lived with Memme and Tätä and my cat Tondu. There had been rooms full of furniture and walls with pictures on them. There had been a Blue Room and a Music Room. But my favourite place was the kitchen table by the window, where I sat and waited. I waited for Mimma and Taat to visit us from Tallinn, the capital, 100 kilometres away. Mother and Father lived in the theatre, so I couldn't live with them. I waited for snow. Then for the snow to melt. I waited for spring. Then for summer.

Memme and Tätä were very 'spiritual'. Tätä played the piano most of the time, because 'music was her life', when she wasn't going to the well or sweeping the path. She also gave music lessons and 'concerts' on the promenade on summer Sunday afternoons, when she wore her hairpiece. She never married, and Memme was a widow. Grandpa had been a well-known Estonian poet and had died young, 'as befitted his soul,' said Memme, every time we placed flowers under his cherry tree, planted over his grave, or rested at the foot of his statue in the town square.

When Tätä made her daily trips to the well, I watched her progress through the misted window, there and back, and it drew a circle in my mind. The circle was closed and snug. In the winter she slid along the path with just her head above the snow banks, buckets clanking at the handles. She went in a gust of cold air and snowflakes, a body tightly wrapped in scarves and overcoat, topped by an apron tied around with string. She turned the winch slowly, blowing on one cold hand and then the other, and stamping her felt boots on the snow as the bucket went down and came up again. And when she re-entered the kitchen and had completed the circle, she had completed my existence as well. As I nibbled on a piece of salt herring, it really didn't matter that the war had begun, that Russians were camping at the bottom of our garden and had taken over the Blue Room and the rest of the house, and were thumping on Tätä's piano.

But it wasn't always winter, and the Russians didn't stay very long. There were long summers after that. Memme and I sketched together on the side porch, while Tätä played Chopin again or Tchaikovsky. There was always a breeze from the sea that lifted the edge of my drawing paper, pushed the curtains out the windows, and chased away the gnats.

Mostly we sketched the tall poplars at the end of the garden overlooking the lagoon. They were so tall, I wondered if you could see them from Finland or Sweden. We sketched them because Memme said no matter how many times you try to draw a tree, it will always come out differently. Each time you will see something new in it. 'To capture the personality of a tree is the most difficult thing in the world, next to drawing people's hands.'

Then, suddenly, I would feel a silence all around me, and there was Mrs Vallas standing patiently beside my desk in the schoolroom, waiting for an answer.

What had been the question?

That was one of the drawbacks to games like 'imagination'. One minute you'd be skipping under a cherry tree on a poet's grave or trying to remember what your father looked like, and the next you'd be standing in a corner of the classroom with your face to the wall.

But even the wall could be turned into a secret garden of blue butterflies and pollen-dusted bumblebees.

As soon as the class returned to 'My name is Mary. What is your name?' the pictures returned. And we had a 'natural' garden, as Memme called it, after the thaw and the flood. And we had gooseberry bushes, red-currant bushes, black-currant bushes, a thatch of horseradish, and some vegetables. The ants ate most of the vegetables, and the rest were made a meal of by one thing or another. Memme handed me Grandpa's magnifying glass so I could see the caterpillars munching, the beetles crunching. Dragonflies hung over the horseradish, and fat bumblebees bumped their sides together in the flowers by the fence, between the white nettles and the stinging nettles that Memme cooked into nettle soup.

But the best time was the early morning, when the spider webs still sparkled with raindrops and dew, because that was when the blue butterflies were born. I missed the blue butterflies most, although they had upset me. They only lived one day and died at sunset. Tätä slipped on the ice that last winter, and hurt her leg. It got worse and worse until it got 'thrombosed' and when it was time to leave she couldn't come with us. We left her at the gate. She was staying, she said, to change her bandages and to remain with her beloved piano.

I missed a lot of things. Having lost them so abruptly and so completely was like a deep pain. It was like having left food on my plate when I had had enough of it, and thinking about it later when I was starving, and wishing I could go back and finish that meal. But I couldn't.

4 Goat Among the Swans

Winter had entered the camp, and there was no doubt about it. The abandoned fields had a grey frost on them. The soil had turned hard and was moulded into deep ruts and plough lines. Most of the ploughing had been left unfinished. The Germans didn't come back to those fields anymore, after the raid.

My summer path was bleak and bare with not a bit of green on it. A lacy pattern of frosty twigs and branches and spiky grasses pointed at the sky and the last of the crows. My breath was icy, like smoke. I pretended to be a dragon.

Real smoke was wafting in from beyond the camp. The German farmers were burning leaves and stubble on the fields beyond the boundary and letting us know that, for us, there wouldn't be another harvest to steal. As if we were all thieves and robbers. Maybe we were. There was still 'us' and 'them'. At least that hadn't changed.

But at school a new teacher was waiting for us. We were going to take ballet with Madame Maleskaya.

Madame Maleskaya never opened her eyes all morning. She talked with her hands. We were going to put on a show for Christmas. All the classrooms were going to join in together, and it would be 'Bolshoi', whatever that meant. She then opened her eyes to audition the dancers.

At last my big moment had come, I thought. I had never had a chance to go on the stage with my mother and father, but unknown to anyone else, a great dancer was waiting inside me, waiting to be discovered. And I was going to be famous and maybe become the greatest dancer in the world!

The bigger girls from the other classrooms stood aloof from us in little groups, whispering excitedly. We were all watching the teacher, waiting to be called one by one to balance along a raised bench and jump off gracefully at the other end.

There was no doubt about it, my bones had become fluid. My flesh was nothing. Given the chance, I could fly like a bird! I felt as light as a dandelion seed parachuting down the wind.

When my turn came, I climbed up, still full of that feather lightness of flesh and bone, though the excitement had made my knees a bit unsteady.

At the teacher's direction, I spread my wings ... my arms ... and held the position. Holding, holding ... holding ... The bench began to wobble, but still holding desperately, I managed to take to the air. I was soaring in my mind, but landed with a thump. The class burst into laughter.

Madame Maleskaya was very kind. 'Don't worry,' she said, 'you did very well.'

But I knew I hadn't. And she didn't get a chance to see my talent at all, though it was brimming out all over me. The bench had been against me too. It was too narrow and the floorboards were too slack, making me go bump.

I was not chosen for the ballet. Erika was not chosen either. But most of the big girls were.

When I got home I told Memme it wasn't fair.

Memme didn't look up from her cooking. She told me to take off my muddy clogs and put them in front of the stove to be scraped.

'They couldn't see what a good dancer I am.'

'Wait till you're bigger.'

'Who can wait that long!'

It was time to search out Väino. I knocked on his door as softly as I could. Väino understood at once what it was like for a great talent to go unrecognized. He dealt with the same problem every day, with his actors. He had tried to put on a ballet in the theatre under his mother's bed – actually a cardboard box to some people – but not one of his dolls had any talent for the dance. They were all stiff and clumsy, he complained bitterly. And he was definitely going to burn the theatre down.

I suggested we sneak up to the attic and put on our own show. There was a solid ramp under the window with a raised platform that would make a wonderful stage. First I would dance, then Väino. Väino was going to become a theatre director when he grew up, like my father. And he was already training me to become a great actress.

I climbed onstage first. Väino was the audience.

As soon as the audience saw me, they sent up a roar and started clapping and stamping their feet. 'Take a bow and throw kisses,' shouted Väino from the floor. Then he directed me to lift my skirt and show my panties, like a real dancer. He said he knew because his mother and an uncle had taken him to a show once, in Hamburg. The men had all whistled and shouted he said, while the dancer took her clothes off.

This was news to me. On the pictures, the ballerinas had looked all serene. But if Väino had seen it with his own eyes, then he must be right. I tried to do as he told me. I pulled my panties off and held my skirt up high.

'That's right!' shouted Väino, and the audience went wild.

In a frenzy, I put all my frustrations into the dance. Twirling, kicking, jumping, and stamping, I pounded the attic platform from one end to the other. The solid floor groaned and quaked as the dust rose out of the old timbers and tickled my throat and made me choke. Perspiration ran down my nose and into my eyes, but I continued bravely. 'The show must go on,' my mother always said. But I wondered just a little at the back of my mind how the class would cope with such dancing, and felt that it might have been just as well I wasn't chosen for the school ballet – I wouldn't last!

All everybody talked about was the school ballet, while all I could think about was Christmas.

I woke up one morning to a different light in the room. With a great leap of joy, I was out of bed and in front of the window. 'It's snowing, it's snowing,' I shouted and rushed about the room. I wanted to tell Unki, but Memme said better not. Unki had only been in bed for about an hour.

No lingering this morning. Memme couldn't dress me quickly enough. She put on at least three of everything. Lastly came the hat over my ears, which she tied down with a scarf. I was so bundled up I couldn't look over my shoulder.

As Unki was asleep, I let Memme wind the rags around my feet. This time they were necessary. Over the rags went a pair of her own stockings and, on top of them, the canvas clogs. She let me go with a heavy sigh.

'Don't get wet,' she called after me, knowing full well that I would.

The field path had disappeared. There was just a white landscape. The snowstorm continued, and I could barely see where the road ended and the fields began. But I didn't want to go the long way around. I didn't want to be late for the snowball fights in the school yard. Later the snow would be slushy or be cleared away by the caretaker.

Taking a general bearing by the church spire, I stumbled on, sometimes up to my chest. The wooden soles attracted the snow. I kept growing taller and taller until I fell down. So I made a game of it, to see how high I could grow before I tumbled.

Linda's mother called from the window to tell Mrs Vallas that Linda was still too sick to come to school and might not come again till spring.

As soon as I approached the school yard, I could see the fights were well under way. The Lithuanians were pelting the Latvians and the Latvians were pelting the Estonians. I was all set to take up my position on the right flank when I remembered my errand. But I couldn't find Mrs Vallas anywhere.

By the time I did find her, she was ringing the school bell. And so I missed the action. All because of Linda. She *would* have to be sick again, on the day of the first snow!

The benches were half empty. Some pupils didn't have coats, and others didn't have proper shoes. They didn't have blankets to make suits out of or Unkis who knew how to wind rags around their feet.

Instead of going to classes we were herded into a hall and told to sit at long tables for a special breakfast. Nobody knew what to expect, and when it came it was strange and the 'porridge' tasted awful. It was made from 'oats', the teacher told us, and was supposed to be good. The 'cocoa' tasted much better. I guessed this was an English breakfast. Mother had written in her last letter that she ate 'cornflakes' and 'porridge', and she had included a few cornflakes in the envelope. And of course in England they ate white bread all the time.

Madame Maleskaya, who Memme said had really been a great dancer once, rehearsed the Christmas show again, while I chased nasty words out of my mind. Väino had been wrong. And I nearly cried when I saw the costumes, just as in the pictures she had shown us. Short flared muslin skirts, made out of flour bags. But when the dancers twirled, the skirts became wings.

I tried to put the show out of my mind and was thinking that this year maybe we would have a real Christmas (though Memme said we could never have a Christmas like the ones we had in Estonia). Then Madame Maleskaya said she had a surprise for us. We were going to be in the show too.

I sprang forward, but the joy was short-lived. We were going to dance, all right, a dance called 'Little Goats'.

I was chosen to be a goat.

'Kick your heels, little ones,' called Madame from the piano. 'One, two, three! Now shake your horns.' And then we shook our tails.

Memme spent all week sewing my costume, with horns and a tail. Unki said I looked like a little devil in it. Memme blinked at him to 'hush'. So Unki got up to go into the forest, alone. He wouldn't take me with him, but I didn't complain. I knew he was getting some wood to make me a sled for Christmas and was choosing a good Christmas tree that he could chop down later.

When the big night arrived, Memme put on her best scarf, pulled a pencil across her eyebrows, and said she was ready.

The 'theatre' was next to the schoolhouse. It was really the church hall, but everybody was calling it 'the theatre' already. We went the long way around and met lots of people on the road, all going the same way. It was a clear, frosty night. We could hear them laughing. Memme carried my goat outfit.

Mrs Peterson was right behind us, wearing her best scarf too. Mrs Ott was hobbling painfully beside her in her silver wedding slippers and holding on to Mrs Peterson's arm, it was so slippery. I felt like running from one to the other and calling, 'Hello, hello!' And I wondered if Mrs Ott was going to fall.

There was a strong whiff of mothballs as soon as we entered the hall. Chairs had been placed in rows before a real stage. There were lights everywhere. Everybody had come to see the ballet, I thought sourly.

Memme chose a seat, and I was led backstage to be dressed. The goat dance was to be the first, followed by the ballet. Erika was a goat too. I knew how she felt!

We were all accounted for and waiting in the wings for the curtain to rise. All the parents were out in front. The audience was shifting on the other side of the curtain getting fidgety – blowing their noses, coughing, searching for their glasses, trying to read the handwritten programmes we had laboured over for a week. And it was all real, not just in my imagination.

Like a shot from a pistol, the order came. 'Go on!'

There was no time to think, just throw myself onstage, one-two-three! Blinded and stunned by the lights, one-two-three, I collided with Erika, who was going the wrong way, one-two-three-hop! Then back into the wings. It was all over! And my only impression had been of lights, music, and heads like rows of cabbages on a moonlit field.

Then the lights dimmed. The music changed. It was time for the ballet. The dancers glided out onto the stage, like swans over water. The music was familiar. Tätä used to play it all the time on her piano. The feeling of lost time came back with an image of billowing curtains. Voices in the living room ... Mother coming into my room to see if I was still awake ... a tall man's shadow in the doorway, in an evening cape ... They had just arrived by train, and we were going back the next day to spend a week on the farm. I felt tears come to my eyes and put my fingers in my ears until the dance was over.

Memme and the other parents came backstage to congratulate us. Memme's cheeks were wet. She said I did well but that she had been looking at my costume and found that one horn was shorter than the other.

Memme and I went home together, the long way around again. Memme had difficulty walking in her old high-heeled galoshes and held on to my shoulder for support. As we passed Number Two we heard loud singing from inside.

'They are brewing Christmas ale,' said Memme with a sigh.

At home it was dark. There was no need to ask where Unki was. I could tell by Memme's face. I wanted to stay up and wait for him. I wanted to tell him about the ballet. But Memme wouldn't let me. 'To bed at once,' she said, sounding sterner than usual. Her mouth was tightly drawn. I knew what to expect.

Around midnight, Unki returned. He was drunk and woke everybody in the house and didn't even stop shouting when he entered our room. Instead of singing he was angry. He said everybody was evil. 'Liars and cheats!' And he said he was going to kill himself right away. He opened his knife and waved it around the room.

'Liars and cheats,' he shouted.

Memme was strangely quiet. I stayed under the blankets, but peeped out anyway to see what was happening. As Unki staggered into his chamber, Memme went after him and sat down next to him on the bed.

'I'll kill myself!' said Unki.

'All right,' said Memme. 'But why don't you rest a bit first? Then you'll have more strength. Why, that knife looks so blunt it wouldn't cut butter!'

Unki agreed, and quieted down a bit. He saw me watching from the bed. He came over and lifted me into his arms and held me close to his chest.

'They're all liars and cheats except you, Rin-Tin-Tin,' he said. 'I love you!' His chin scratched, but I kissed him too.

Memme was right there. 'Tomorrow you'll feel much better, Paul.' She helped him back to bed. Unki was snoring almost before his head touched the pillow.

5 Christmas

All at once it was Christmas Eve!

Luckily I had another friend, an old gentleman with a horse and cart. He made daily trips to Stadthagen town centre for a special fine bread called 'sepik' and for lemonade, which he sold in the camp. He let me ride with him when I asked nicely, and I called him my 'Sepik Uncle'.

It was much better than hanging on to the back of the food truck. We 'chatted', with a piece of warm sepik bread in one hand and an open bottle of lemonade in the other. The horse plodded along in a steady creaking of harness. The cart rattled; the lemonade bottles chimed in their crates.

Because it was Christmas, the load was twice as big. The lemonade bottles had Christmas in them that evening. The warm sepik loaves were wrapped in sacking. We had Lebkuchen – honey cake – and sweets as well. And a box of silver stars. My fingers itched to pick one up and twirl it by the string. But Sepik Uncle said No. He said they were for sale and customers would not buy goods that had been 'fingered'.

Sepik Uncle was sitting quietly, reins in hand, watching the road. I was used to his not talking much. When we chatted it was more like me thinking aloud. 'One, two, three.' I tried to dangle my legs in rhythm with the horse's hooves. It was not easy, seeing it had four legs and I only two.

It was very cold. Even the air seemed frozen. My breath made a white curtain, like Memme's cheesecloth, before my eyes. The sky was getting darker.

Memme was expecting me home soon. But I had to give her time to finish putting up the tree and to cut candles, sort presents, and get out the family photographs.

I was not to expect a tree that would brush the ceiling, or one that would be loaded down with dazzling ornaments and sparkling tinsel. I was not to expect presents to be piled halfway up the tree or to be taken to church for the Christmas service, wrapped in a fur blanket on Tambu Papa's sleigh. All that had been a dream.

But still there was always to be some kind of tree, even a small branch would do with a candle. Even in the air-raid shelter, Memme had lighted a candle 'to bring in the light'. The Germans, too, had lighted candles, when we all huddled in the wet mountain shelter. And for once they had not minded that we were foreigners, as we sang 'Silent Night' together. Outside the bombs had been falling, falling like Christmas candles.

But last year Memme had baked a cake and got a tree, and this year it was going to be even better. I knew it, because parcels had been arriving from England and disappearing mysteriously. And Unki had been hammering and sawing in his chamber for the past few weeks.

I wondered if Memme had finished. What if she was already waiting?

The road from Stadthagen to the camp was deep in snow. It seemed endless. But as we neared the first house, all the lights were on. I glanced down to the right to see if our light was on. It was hard to tell.

Sepik Uncle had a long list of customers, but no one in Number One. We didn't even stop by the brewery. The singing was twice as loud as usual. Unki was there. Perhaps he, too, was waiting for Memme to get everything ready.

At Number Three, the people were already out on the road, and hailed us from a distance. Everybody was in good humour. But you could never tell. There was Mrs Vallas, whose smile of welcome took on a shade of annoyance when she saw me. What was I doing out so late? Why wasn't I at home with my grandmother? I needed a stronger hand, more discipline – you know, the usual! Still, I couldn't help but think of Memme once more. Supposing she was waiting for me, with the candles cut and ready to be lighted.

At Number Four redhead Pügi's mother bought a loaf of sepik and three silver stars. There were just six left.

The yellowish light from the windows reflected on the snow. The shadows became deeper and bluer. I felt the Christmas spirit in every house, and again it made me think of Memme. I must go home, I thought. The warm bread and the merry bottles no longer charmed me so much. At Number Four, in a downstairs window, I saw a huge Christmas tree with the candles lighted. It must be time.

Mrs Roog, one of Memme's friends, sent her best wishes. She looked at me questioningly. What was I doing there on Christmas Eve?

Sepik Uncle read off the list. Two bottles of lemonade, two loaves of sepik, a box of Lebkuchen, and two stars. Four more stars to go. If only I had some money!

At House Number Seven, I decided I must go home now. So I jumped off the cart before I could change my mind. Sepik Uncle grabbed my sleeve. 'Merry Christmas!' he said. I had forgotten my manners completely.

'And a Merry Christmas to you too,' I said quickly, and did a curtsy. 'I must go home now. Thank you for the ride.'

Sepik Uncle smiled and reached under the seat. 'Take this to your grandmother with my compliments,' he said, handing me a warm sepik. His fingers moved on to the box. 'And this is for you.' It was one of the silver stars.

My wish had come true! I made another curtsy and gave Sepik Uncle a big kiss. I let the star twirl on the string before stuffing it in my trouser leg. As I didn't have pockets, I always used my trouser leg for safekeeping.

With the bread securely under my arm, I waved good-bye to

Sepik Uncle, his horse and cart, and set off by the field path towards home. It would be quicker than along the main road. I jumped the ditch and started running as fast as I could. I was in a white world, alone at the crossroads. The devil would not get me tonight – not at Christmas. Memme said he spends his Christmas at the brewery.

It had been weeks since I came that way, and there had been many snowstorms since. I hadn't realized the snow was so deep. And I hadn't noticed that it was getting completely dark. Unki always says, 'Who the devil knows the devil?' Could he not be in two places at once? Waiting outside the brewery and at the crossroads as well?

As the ditches were level with the path, I could not see where they started or ended. I couldn't see where I was stepping. Before long I was up to my chest in snow.

As I struggled out of the ditch, I promised myself never to stay out this late again. I got out all right, only to find that I had left the bread behind. There was nothing else to do but go back for it. Tears turned hard on my cheeks. My clothes were getting stiff. The loaf of sepik was soaked through, so I put it inside my jacket.

Running, falling, stumbling, and running again! The bread began to fall apart. All I had left were two squashy pieces. Then an awful thought flashed through my head. With trembling, frozen fingers, I lifted my trouser leg. The star was safe!

The star was for Memme. It was my Christmas present for her. At school, I had been forced to make her a pincushion, not because I wanted to but because I had to, so it didn't count. Besides, it was really a bit tattered and stained with bloody pinpricks.

I spun the star around once more, to be sure it still worked, and polished it with my sleeve. I was almost home. Lights were burning in the distance. Number Sixteen was straight ahead. It was time to straighten my clothes a bit. My braids were undone, so I stuffed them under my hat. My clothes were soaking wet. The blanket cloth was getting stiffer and stiffer, but that was nothing new. I came home this way every evening. Memme just placed me in front of the stove and scraped the ice off with a knife.

A new snowstorm was beginning. The first flakes started to fall, swirling through the air and sliding down my collar. They were looking for warmth, like moths and butterflies that fly into light bulbs, 'to die', Memme says. 'Life and death go hand in hand, as do joy and sorrow.'

As I got closer to the light, I got a shock. That wasn't Number Sixteen. I had never seen that particular house before. I was in the German section of the village. Number Sixteen was as far from there as it had been from the crossroads where I started!

My feet were tired.

It would have been nice to sit down in the soft snow and have a little rest. But I knew I mustn't. A friend of Unki's had done that and had frozen to death. He had been drunk, of course, 'and didn't feel a thing,' said Unki.

Various stories came to mind. There was the little girl who had fallen asleep in the snow and gone straight to heaven. I thought I would rather get back home first. And that boy who went into the forest to look for a Christmas tree and never came back. And the little beggar girl with the matches. They all had died! I struggled on.

New lights ahead! That had to be Number Sixteen. But it could also be a 'fantamogosma' or something. Unki had told me about those. They appeared in deserts mostly. You could look out over the sand, and whole cities would appear from nowhere. But these weren't really there, and you never reached them.

I trudged into the yard, and recognized Leena's red curtains, which had been babushka's underskirt before.

How easy it was to walk on the hard-packed snow. I should have gone the long way around. It would have been simpler. But as soon as I entered Number Fifteen, everything was forgotten but Memme.

I burst into the room. It was dark. Memme was sitting by the window. She was waiting. I ran to her and put my head on her lap. I was home.

Memme's lap was warm. Her chest was soft and smelled of cooking and baking.

'I thought of going to look for you. Where have you been so long?' She stroked my wet hair. But I felt she wasn't really thinking about me. Cat was sleeping, curled up beside the stove.

'I came as quickly as I could.'

Memme sighed. 'You didn't see your Uncle Paul in the village, did you?'

But just then the door opened, and Unki staggered in. He put his palms up and said, 'I'm not drunk. Just a little on the nose.' A Christmas-tree stand was under his arm. That was why Memme had been waiting. She couldn't put up the tree without the stand.

Unki went to his chamber to get a hammer and nails. And then he went to get the tree from the pigsty, where it was standing in a bucket of water.

Memme switched on the electric light bulb and got busy. The candles had been cut, six small ones from two big ones.

While Unki hammered and sawed, Memme undressed me. She dried my hair first. When I took off my jacket, a big handful of bread crumbs fell on the floor. The sepik! But Memme didn't ask what it was, and there was no point in explaining about something that no longer existed.

Memme draped my wet suit on the stovepipe to dry.

With a warm blanket around me, I ate supper. I would rather have started on the cake that I could see was wrapped up and hidden in Memme's bed, under the blanket, or on the oranges and chocolates that I could smell somewhere else in the room. Memme's blanket was pulled way down in front. Since we had no cupboards or any other furniture except for the beds, bench, table, and chair, I guessed they were under Memme's bed, along with other things I wasn't supposed to see yet.

I watched Unki setting up the tree. It was a good-sized tree, though it didn't reach to the ceiling. It had firm branches and only a slight bald spot, which Unki turned to the wall.

Because it was supposed to be a surprise, I closed my eyes while Unki lighted the candles. He was the 'master of the house' now, and everything that happened, happened according to custom. It was all a part of the tradition, which never changed and which had made our Christmases the same in spirit no matter where we were. I knew the customs. Still, I couldn't help but remember that in Estonia, I had been led in from another room, so I could gasp in surprise at the splendid sight.

To keep my mind on the 'spirit' and with my eyes still shut, I said a quick prayer to Jesus, thanking him for not making Memme angry because I had been late and wet and for keeping me safe from the devil. Unki too.

'You can look now,' said Memme.

The candles were lighted. Memme switched off the light bulb and I went to sit next to her on the bed. The tree was beautiful. I tried not to think that it looked a bit bare, and that the room seemed a bit empty without Mother and – But there they were! Memme had pinned their pictures to the wallpaper!

That, too, was a part of the custom. We would talk about them and place them under the tree later. And I would think about Tondu.

Suddenly I remembered my star!

I rushed frantically over to the stovepipe and grabbed my steaming trousers, groped about in the leg. It was there! The corners were a trifle wilted and it was kind of soft, but otherwise it was all right.

I stood in front of Memme and pressed the star into her palm. Then I put my arms around her neck and kissed her. 'Merry Christmas, Memme!'

Memme gathered me close and called Unki. Unki lifted me up

and let me fasten the star to the tip of the tree. He said it was just what we needed. Memme thought so too. The silver paper star shone like a real star, reflecting the candlelight. There were two Christmas trees and two stars – one in the room and another in the windowpane, against the night sky.

As I sat in Memme's lap, we began the ceremony that Memme said had been a part of her childhood and her mother's childhood and her grandmother's before that.

Unki sat at the table. His arms hung heavy by his side. He had a headache.

First we looked at the candles for a while in silence.

'The light came out of the darkness,' said Memme at last. Her arms were warm around me. Then she started singing 'Silent Night', her eyes closed, her voice thin and trembly. I dared not sing, but Unki joined in with a deep rumble. Then Memme reached for her Bible and read the first lines that opened to her hand.

'He brought me also out of the horrible pit, out of the mire and clay, and set my feet upon the rock, and ordered my goings. Amen.' Then she added, 'I find that prophetic!' She sounded pleased.

It was time to talk about the family, 'those who are near in spirit also and dear to us but who cannot be with us this evening'.

First Mimma. Memme placed her picture under the tree, propped against a cigar box. She said she hoped we would join her soon in England.

Then came my father's picture, which was a bit blurred. He had just turned his head. 'God guide his conscience,' said Memme shortly.

Tätä's picture was pressed silently to her bosom. Memme couldn't trust herself to speak. Tears rolled down her cheeks.

My other grandparents, Tambu Mamma and Grandpappy, stared at us sternly from their farmhouse parlour. Grandpappy was dead, but Mamma had 'not been heard from'. That usually meant Siberia. I remembered Grandpappy's funeral. I had found him sleeping in the parlour in a long box. 'Get up, Grandpappy,' I said. 'Let's play!' But he had his best suit on and he couldn't.

There followed a long list of relatives whose names I had heard every Christmas although I didn't know who they were, and who were 'all thinking of us, as we think of them, at this holy hour'.

And I thought of my former cat Tondu, as I had meant to.

When Tätä had been rehearsing or giving piano lessons, we had always been together, Memme, Tondu, and I. When it had rained or it was too cold to go outside, we'd sat at the kitchen table, and Memme had taught us how to make up poems. Mine were about things like tall poplars or the blue butterflies, or about a fly with a thousand eyes. Tondu's poems were mainly about birds and fish. When the full moon rose above the lagoon, Tondu climbed up to the roof of the woodshed and sat inside the moon, for hours. Tondu knew about 'spiritual' life too, but more than anything he liked to eat fish.

And it was over fish that I lost him.

It happened that last spring. As usual in spring, our cellar was flooded. Mimma came from Tallinn for a visit and brought us a smoked eel. To keep it fresh, Tätä lowered it into the cellar and hung it on a nail just above the waterline.

It wasn't long before I saw Tondu pawing at the cellar window from the outside. He had smelled the fish, and had already opened the shutters. He knew that I had seen him but then guessed rightly that I didn't mind.

I didn't mind at all. I even helped him by removing the peg from the latch. But I had forgotten about the water.

We were in the kitchen having supper, when we heard a strange noise. A sort of mouse sound, only it was a meow. It was coming from under the kitchen floor. Right away I remembered the eel. I ran outside to the cellar window. The window was open, and I looked inside. On the highest cellar step, with the water lapping at his tail, was Tondu. He had managed to swim across and was shivering and crying under the kitchen trapdoor. The eel was hanging about a foot away from him, still out of reach.

Tondu heard me because he looked back. I'll never forget that look! And he spat at me, three times.

Mimma opened the trapdoor and lifted Tondu out. He was wrapped in a warm towel. Memme mixed some valerian tea with his milk, to calm his nerves. Tondu looked so thin, even his whiskers were flat. We stroked and petted him until he purred again, but not for me. Never again did he purr for me. He blamed me for the accident. He thought I had let him jump into the water on purpose.

When we left Estonia, he didn't even come to the gate to say good-bye.

'And those who have passed on to another life will be with us anyway,' said Memme, coming to the end of her list.

'Amen!'

Unki shifted on the bench.

Silence once again filled the room. The candles flickered in the draught from the window. We didn't have curtains.

But I knew what was coming next! The moment I had been waiting for. The presents!

Unki mumbled something about being chilly and went into his chamber. Memme followed.

Memme came out first and scattered an armful of parcels on my bed.

'A Merry Christmas!' she said, and sat on a corner of the mattress to watch me. She dabbed her eyes with her apron and was 'moved'.

Unki was stuck in the doorway of his chamber with something big. The sled! But I must not help. Not yet. I wasn't supposed to know. Finally he navigated it through the door and placed it in the middle of the room. 'Merry Christmas, Rin-Tin-Tin!' He grinned. 'And don't break your neck.'

On the side of the sled was painted 'Lotukata' in red letters.

'Oh, Unki!' I jumped up and hugged him until he pleaded for mercy. 'Don't strangle me!'

Memme lifted her bedspread and placed everything on the table. It was a sight to behold! And there were more parcels on my bed.

From Mimma, I got a big rubber ball, some English books, and a flashlight with batteries that flashed three different colours.

From Memme, a woollen cardigan, a pair of gloves, a drawing block and pencils, and a box of water colours.

The biggest parcel was still in its brown wrapping, as it had come from the post office. Even Memme didn't know what was in it.

We gathered around, and Unki helped me to undo the strings. He cut them with his penknife. Memme shook her head. She said he would never make a good husband because cutting the string was a sign of impatience.

In the parcel was a pair of boy's boots with hooks and metal cleats! From my mother. Now I could 'strike fire', as I had seen boys do in Hausberge, by striking the metal heels against the cobblestones, so that sparks flew out both sides. With boots like this, I thought, Rein might even promote me to major!

Memme and Unki admired them too.

'Good and watertight,' said Memme.

'Expensive leather,' said Unki, smelling them. 'Much better than mine!'

Memme gathered up my wooden clogs and stuffed them in the stove.

But what about my presents to them! I had almost forgotten. I groped around inside my mattress for the pincushion and

Unki's scarf. I had knitted it especially for him. Mrs Kuimets, the other teacher we had, said it was too narrow and too short, but Unki liked it. He said it was just what he wanted, as I wrapped it around his neck. He kept it on.

Memme thought the pincushion was 'so artistic'. She stuck a pin in it right away for 'safekeeping'. Usually when Memme put a thing somewhere for safekeeping, she never found it again.

It was time to turn to the cake and biscuits, the oranges and chocolates. And to munch for a while. And to look pleased.

The stove hissed and spat embers across the room, and Unki had to keep getting up to stamp them out. 'I must tack some tin under the stove,' he remembered. The clogs were not burning too well.

Cat stirred in her sleep. Her whiskers were itching, and no doubt her fur was getting hot. She was probably dreaming she was a young kitten again, chasing her own tail.

The candles were getting lower. The room got darker and darker. With my stomach full and my eyes half closed, I watched the last candle go out in a wisp of smoke. 'It will be an eventful year,' noted Memme. The last candle held great significance for her.

Outside a group of drunks passed by. Unki shifted uneasily again but pretended he hadn't heard. He yawned, stretched, mumbled something about 'tomorrow's light' also coming, and walked slowly to his chamber.

Memme continued sitting in the dark, humming to herself, 'Lo, how a rose e'er blooming.' It had been Tätä's favourite carol.

I gathered Cat up from the hot floorboards and climbed on Memme's lap. 'Memme,' I asked, 'why can't we go back to Haapsalu? I thought the war was over.'

'It's a long story,' said Memme. 'When you're bigger, you'll understand.'

'But I want to understand now,' I pleaded. 'And now I'm bigger than last year. You said the same thing then.'

Memme sat still a minute, then pulled Cat and me closer and said, 'I'll tell you a story instead. It's about a little Estonian girl called Aino.

'It was Christmas Eve. Aino lived in a DP camp in Germany with her mother and ...'

'With her grandmother,' I prompted quickly. Memme's stories were much better when they included her and me.

'All right, with her grandmother. It was Christmas Eve. Santa was reading his long, long list of all the presents he was going to deliver that night, to all the children in the whole world. But when he came to the name Aino, he stopped. She had not asked for anything. A little girl who did not want Christmas presents, that he had to see! So he hopped into his sleigh, whipped up his reindeer, and before you could say "Merry Christmas", he had landed in the camp and was talking to Aino, the little girl who did not want any Christmas presents. "But surely you would like a doll," said Santa. He could see that Aino had no dolls, no toys of any kind. The room was bare and sparsely furnished. "Or maybe a doll's house,' suggested Santa, "full of furniture." But Aino shook her head, "You must want something," said Santa.

'"Oh, I do," said Aino. "I want to go home for Christmas."

'"But that's impossible," said Santa. "Everything else I can give you, but I can't give you that."

'"Just for a few hours," pleaded Aino. "We could be back before morning."

'Santa had never been unable to please a little girl in his lifetime. A sad little girl made him sad too. So Santa said "All right, but only for a few hours."

'And they set off for Estonia in Santa's sleigh. Over the snow they went and as far as they could go, until they arrived in the little seaside town of Haapsalu.'

Memme paused for breath.

'I want Aino to live with her Memme, and Tätä too, and have a cat called Tondu,' I injected hastily.

'All in good time,' said Memme. 'Now listen on.'

'Aino and Santa went on through the town. And it was just as Aino had remembered it. There were the castle ruins, by the open-air market. There was the railway station where Aino had last seen her father off on a train to Tallinn. There was the milk ship where Aino and her grandmother used to buy milk. And there was the Promenade, the hotel, and Aino's grandfather's statue.

'And there they were coming to the mud-bath sanatorium and Aino recognized her own street. And the boat yard. And the lagoon.'

She's coming to it, I thought suddenly. And I felt a surge of excitement and panic. I remembered it was sixteen fence rails to our gate. I sat forward on Memme's lap. She continued.

'As Aino passed the sanatorium, she noticed that all the mud barges were stuck in the ice untended. But she couldn't see the poplars, because it was dark and had started snowing. She held Santa's hand as they approached the gate. The house was as she remembered it, set back from the road. But there were no lights on. Not even in the kitchen window. Everything looked deserted. There were not even any footprints in the snow between the gate and the porch.'

I bit my lip. Tätä had always cleared a path, no matter how deep the snow was, so she could get to the well.

'No one came to the door,' said Memme. 'The house was deserted.'

'Not even a black cat?' I asked.

'Not even a cat,' said Memme.

'Nobody?'

'Well,' agreed Memme after a pause. 'Aino did think she saw a cat's face in the kitchen window, but it was dark and snowing. There was just a hint of white whiskers. Aino was just about to open the gate when she heard barking, and a mean dog came tearing around the house. It almost bit Aino's hand. This strange dog was guarding the house and would not let Aino enter. "It's no use," said Santa. "No one lives here anymore, and the dog won't let you pass. We will have to go back."

'But Aino wouldn't hear of it yet. "My father lives in Tallinn," she said, "in an apartment near the theatre. Maybe Tätä and Tondu went to live with him." Santa, being Santa, said all right. "But it is getting late. I have a lot of toys to deliver by morning."

'By magic – and magic it was – they soon found themselves in Tallinn, outside a big modern apartment building. Aino had only been there a few times, but she remembered the number of the apartment. Santa said he would wait outside in the sleigh.

'Aino went up the stairs and rang the bell of Number 21 on the second floor. At first there was no answer, but after a minute, she heard a man's voice. Her father's! Footsteps came down the passage, and someone was grumbling and fumbling at the locks. The door opened eventually, and a strange woman stood there, staring down at Aino very annoyed. "What do you want?" asked the woman, whom Aino had never seen before. Looking past her, Aino could see her father sitting in the living room with his back to the door, reading a newspaper. She wanted to call out his pet name, "Taat!" but the woman pulled the door closer. "Off with you," she shouted, "and stop bothering the famous theatre director." At that she slammed the door in Aino's face.

'Santa, who had crept up silently behind the girl, put his arms around her and said there was no point in searching any further. It was time to go back to the DP camp. But Aino would not be persuaded. There was one more place left, and she begged Santa to take her to the farm. There was a chance that Tätä and Tondu had gone there as a last resort.

'And it looked as if Aino was right. As soon as Santa reined in the sleigh outside the farmhouse, Aino could see that all the lights were on and that there was a big party going in the parlour. She hurried to the window as fast as she could and saw the room full of people, all standing around and talking and laughing and raising their glasses to each other, just as they used to. On a side table there was Christmas sausage, pork and sauerkraut, and kringel cake. Aino pressed her nose to the window, looking for a familiar face, but she couldn't see one – not even one. She looked at everyone in turn, and once again in panic, but they were all strangers. No one in the house belonged to her or she to them.

'"Come," said Santa, "it's no use. We really must return. There is someone whom you do belong to, who is waiting for you in Germany in the DP camp, someone who loves you very much, and who is getting very anxious."

'There was nothing for it. Aino got into the sleigh and soon found herself back in the little room with her grandmother. And you know what?'

'What?' I asked.

'The room was full of presents. And Aino was so glad to be back with somebody who loved her and to whom she belonged that she thought that was the best present of all.'

Memme had finished her story. But I wasn't satisfied.

'But why, Memme?' I asked.

'Why what?'

'Why couldn't she find anybody home? What happened to them all?'

Memme sighed and held me close. 'You see,' she said, 'a wicked witch came and put Estonia under a spell. And it is still under that spell, from that day to this.'

'Can't anybody break it?'

'No,' said Memme, 'not now. But one day, maybe someone will.'

Christmas morning dawned white and sunny. Icicles dripped off our window ledge and off the edge of the roof. Part of the windowpanes was still milky with frost, but the patterns were breaking, and by the time Memme got me bundled up and had laced my new boots, it had melted away.

The smell of Christmas was still in the room, and the silver star was shining brightly on top of the Christmas tree in the morning sunlight. I had an orange for breakfast and four biscuits, and a glass of hot powdered milk mixed with melted chocolate.

Memme was smiling most of the time and humming little snatches of 'Hallelujah, hall-e-lujah', as she tied my gloves to a piece of string and threaded them through my jacket sleeves. When I was all ready, she gave my boots a coating of pork fat to preserve them.

Unki was still asleep. I'd hoped he would come with me when I took my sled for its first run, but maybe later. There was time enough for once. I had a whole week off from school.

In the hall, Inge and Väino admired my sled – Väino from his doorway. He wasn't allowed out of his room because he had the mumps. Inge showed us her present, a wooden rifle. And Väino's dream had also come true. His mother had bought him a real doll. Its eyes opened and closed. He had already tied strings to its arms and legs. The doll walked beside him.

Memme came downstairs and said to keep away from Väino, that mumps was catching. But Väino's mother had gone out and left him alone. It seemed like the best time for us to get together to play with that doll. And I thought of the fun we would have in the attic.

'Come on, let's go up,' I said.

But Väino dared not. His face was all blown up, and he looked like a ball with handles on the side. There was nothing for me to do but to climb in through the window myself. We played together most of the day and every other day thereafter, when I wasn't sledding. One of his mother's friends had stepped on his theatre and his mother had thrown it out. We started to build a new one from the box in which my boots had come.

Memme said I was a good girl for staying away from Väino, but I got sick anyway. Not the mumps but the 'fevers' that came at night and made the walls pull together, then expand again. I screamed for Memme to help me. She sat on my bed and held a cold spoon to my forehead. She changed the 'compresses' that I hated: I couldn't move and Mrs Ott came in to help wind them around me. Memme's compress bag was famous and Linda's mother borrowed it most of the time. It was full of sheets and rags and old woollen underclothes. They were soaked in hot water and wrapped tightly around my body, with the dry layers on top. Unki said I looked like a 'mummy': an Egyptian mother.

There was no doctor but Memme fed me green cooking apples and they made me well. But I still held Memme's hand before falling asleep, as I had always done, to know that I was safe.

During wartime, Memme always sat by my bed at night and held my hand. We slept fully dressed. Often I woke up in a panic, thinking she had left me, only to find her in her chair asleep. Her hand had slipped from mine.

Memme had taught me a prayer:

> Take me under your wing, oh Jesus.
> Let this little bird be safe.
> If the Devil's flying near,
> Let your angels interfere –
> This child shall sleep in peace. Amen.

The prayers helped. I got well again. But Memme wouldn't let me outside for a long time. Instead we played together in the room, as we had done before we came to the camp. We drew each other, played hide and seek or chased each other around my bed, until Memme threw herself down exhausted. 'I can't any more,' she'd say. Then we'd play something quiet like looking at old photographs and boxes. 'Oh look, dear Ernie's last poem before he died,' and 'here's one of Alma and me at the Seminar!' She'd blow her nose then and wipe her eyes and be happy.

My English books were also waiting to be read, but I couldn't find anyone who could read them to me.

One day Memme came up from the kitchen. She said there

was a young lady in the house who could speak English and would read the books to me. Her name was Klarissa.

I knew Klarissa, I had seen her several times. Very beautiful but quite old. At least twenty. She had stopped to talk to me one day in the yard. Because she was so beautiful I hadn't known what to answer. She asked me the name of my cat and I said, 'Cat'. She had misunderstood me.

It still bothered me. Whenever I saw her I got hot all over and felt so stupid I ran away. When a person is so beautiful, you just can't talk to them.

With hammering heart I collected my books together and went downstairs. I knocked on Klarissa's door ever so softly, hoping she wasn't in. But the door opened at a touch. The room was darkish. There was only one lamp on a table by the bed. I remembered such a lamp from Estonia. It was called a table lamp for 'romantic lighting'.

Klarissa was reclining on the bed, which was more like a heavenly couch really. She looked like a princess. I had entered fairyland. The princess's rose garden. I could actually smell the roses and was overwhelmed by their smell.

Klarissa beckoned me into the light and asked if I was feeling better. 'Such nice books you have there!'

I nodded, afraid of saying something stupid again.

The princess told me not to be afraid, to come forward and make myself comfortable. I had never seen such wonderful hair, except in pictures of Grimm's fairy tales.

'Yes Ma'am,' I managed weakly. I was glued to my place on the floorboards.

She finally took my hand and pulled me forward. To sit on the heavenly couch, next to her. Right up against the smell of roses. I was so happy I could have whooped.

Klarissa selected the first book and started to read. Her voice was sweet and low and somehow smiling. She explained that the story was about an Arab boy called Aladdin, who found a magic lamp.

I couldn't understand a word of what she was reading but the magic of the cave and the lamp were of this room. Snacking tit-bits from a dish beside the 'couch', I knew this magic was for real. It would be wonderful, I thought, if all our English lessons could be like this! The lights could be turned low. Mrs Vallas could splash herself with the scent of roses. We could lie on cushions, pass around tit-bits of dried apples and I felt sure we would learn English much quicker.

Before I knew it, it was New Year's Eve.

Spring 1946 to Autumn 1947

6 The Displaced-Persons Camp

'We are approaching the camp,' said Memme. 'I thought you would want to see.'

I licked my lips – they were dry and cracked – and sat up straight in the jeep. Yes, I remembered. We had left Hausberge at dawn after spending the whole night packing. And now it was nearly noon. Last night we had just sat down to supper when the English jeep had come for us. They hadn't given us much time. And Mimma was sitting in front with the driver, laughing and smoking Camel cigarettes.

I was sitting on top of our red-knitted blanket bundle and holding the baby-blanket bundle on my knee. There was a grey soldier-blanket bundle, a thick UNRRA quilt bundle, Memme's old-coat bundle, and some more of our things tied into smaller bundles. The grey soldier-blanket bundle belonged to Uncle Paul. There wasn't enough room for Unki in the jeep. He was to follow us on his own, later.

The country road was full of potholes. We were somewhere 'near Hanover', said Memme. She had a line of suffering across her forehead, between the tightly wrapped scarf around her mouth and the hat. And she had a pair of dusty eyebrows. Dust was like a mist around us. There was dust in my teeth too. I must have slept a long time, probably with my mouth open.

It was June. I knew that because I was looking forward to my birthday in July. The war had been over for a year, but except for the quietness and the absence of air raids, there hadn't been much peace in Hausberge. There was a lot of 'trouble' and ‘retaliation’, as Memme put it. After the Americans came in and the English took it over as an ‘occupation zone’, we had been awakened night after night by the sound of shots and people running in the street. Several persons had mysteriously disappeared. And others had been blown up by booby traps in the shape of pens and toys left lying in the gutter. I even heard they had found human fingernails in a sausage – a child's fingernails.

Memme wouldn't let me out at all. And nobody went out at night. Most of the shooting was taking place between prisoners released from a nearby concentration camp and former guards, who lived in Hausberge. The Germans were so scared they had started shooting strangers on sight.

Mimma said we would be safe in the DP camp, that the camp was going to be English and that it was especially for people who had nowhere to go like us, because Estonia had now been taken over by the Russians again. She was talking to the driver in English, Memme told me in a whisper. But in the next breath, she whispered to Memme in Estonian out of the side of her mouth. It was something about the Germans. She pointed to the passing fields, and I caught a bit of what she said, although I wasn't meant to. A British pilot had crashed around here somewhere, she said, and the German farmers had pitchforked him to death.

When I heard this, I clutched my baby-blanket bundle a little tighter. The word ‘camp’ had always struck terror in me. Mimma and Memme would whisper at night, while Täta watched the door. People had disappeared into ‘camps’ as long as I could remember. I couldn't see what all the laughing was about now.

The fields on either side were dry and yellow. Last year's wheat was rotting underneath this year's weeds. Everything looked abandoned and ragged, but still it smelled sweetly of hot grass, hay, and poppies. It also smelled of warm gasoline, tar, and dust.

There was war junk in these fields. Overturned jeeps, army trucks, and military ambulances lay there rusting like beetles on their backs. Tank and cannon wrecks were scattered among shells of burned and twisted metal. Some of the vehicles had the American white star on the side, others the British tricolour circle. I knew all the signs by heart. Unki had taught them to me. We had had the same wrecks all around Hausberge, where we used to live, and the same ruins had met us in the small towns we travelled through. Although there was a lot of rebuilding going on, it was all familiar.

'We're nearly there,' said Mother over her shoulder.

'About time.' Memme sighed and pulled her scarf up, hiding everything but her eyes. The jeep bounced over potholes, lifting and landing with bone-shaking jolts. Our bundles rolled this way and that way. We were flung backwards and forwards. All the while Memme, her mouth a thin line under the scarf, was clutching the back of my dress.

The hand on the back of my dress tightened. She must have sensed my apprehension, but also my excitement and desire to stand up and take a look. Memme said we would be eating white bread in this camp, that white bread was much better than rye bread and tasted like cake. I could imagine it already.

'Sit still,' said Memme through her scarf.

But I couldn't. There was a sound. It cut through the summer sky like a scream. Into the ditch! Into the ditch! I jumped to my feet in panic. A plane was approaching, flying low. The jeep bucked, and I stumbled, ready to fling myself over the side. But Memme caught me in her arms. She pressed my face to her dusty bosom.

Nothing happened! No bombs! No strafing!

I lifted my head and realized I had forgotten again that the war was over. We watched the plane till it became a silver dot glinting in the blue and a sweet droning that got weaker and weaker and weaker as it disappeared into the distance. I had never watched a plane before or found it a beautiful sight.

Memme hugged me. I sensed she was smiling behind the scarf.

'There's the camp.' Mother pointed straight ahead.

Memme lowered her scarf to see better. I sat up straight.

We were coming to another village. Just an ordinary village, every bit like Hausberge. German-type farm houses bordered on either side of a fork in the road, each with a large field attached to it. In the distance red roofs huddled together around a church spire, a broken-shafted windmill, and a taller brick building that I guessed was the schoolhouse. There was always a schoolhouse! I had braced myself for anything. Barbed-wire fences. Mud huts, where people froze to death. But not another German village! And not another school full of kids with sharpened pencils!

We reached a fork in the road, which divided two ways. On the corner was the first house, with a big red number *One* printed above the door. Down the right, I could see houses marked *Fifteen* and *Sixteen*.

We drove down the left fork, towards the ruined mill. We passed houses numbered *Two*, *Three*, and *Four*. A man staggered out of Number Two. He waved at us.

I wanted to ask some questions, like where had the pilot landed and what did they do with him after they had pitchforked him? And was his body still out there somewhere? But Memme had a tight-lipped look on her that meant 'Not now'. I think she was a bit miffed because she couldn't understand this English that Mimma and the driver had talked nonstop. Or maybe it was because that drunken man had looked like Unki.

I wished I could speak English. I knew one word, *chocolate*. And I knew *chewing gum* in American.

After Number Five the houses began to come together into a village centre. There was a pavement and people were sunbathing in the garden of Number Eight. They lifted their heads as we drove past. Two girls about my own age ran to the gate and waved. I did not wave back. I had secretly wished there wouldn't be any children in this camp.

The jeep turned into Number Nine with a squeal of tyres.

We had arrived in a quiet farmyard and stopped outside the usual farmhouse front entrance. An old hay wagon stood under the door to the loft, but I could tell at once this wasn't a real farm anymore. The smell was different. There was no straw in the yard and no manure heap. The yard was swept clean. And there were no animals or chickens to be seen or heard.

The driver jumped out of the driver's seat, both feet together. He had red hair cut very short into a brush. I kept looking at him and thinking, 'He is English', as I had stared at the Americans when they had first come, thinking 'They are Americans'. If he'd had three eyes and a nose at the back of his head, I would have believed it. I had heard the words 'English' and 'American' as long as I had heard the word 'camps', and I could tell the difference between the sound of a Russian plane and an American plane. But I couldn't understand how one could be better than the other. The bombs that had come from them had killed all the same.

Mimma eased herself off her seat slowly, rubbing her hips and tugging at her skirt. It was her only one and had a matching jacket with padded shoulders. She had always worn trousers before, and I thought she looked more like her real self than she had for a long time. Even her hair was done up in a roll, instead of being tied back with a kerchief. I often wished my mother were my sister. She looked and acted more like a sister, while Memme acted like a mother. I wished I had a sister or a best friend. Memme was my only friend. She played with me all the time, but sometimes it would have been nice to play with a person my own age. That was impossible, of course. German children didn't like me because I was a foreigner and different, and because their parents didn't like us either.

A woman in a wet apron appeared at the door, shading her eyes against the sun. She stopped when she saw us. Suddenly the yard was full of people, all staring at us, mostly women and children but a few men too, in the background.

Mother threw away her cigarette and disappeared into the house. The driver lifted me down first, then offered Memme his elbow. But she tripped and nearly fell. It was a good thing he caught her. A child tittered, but the sound was abruptly muffled by a mother's hand. I knew everybody was staring at our bundles. No one had ever had so many bundles!

Memme fixed her hat pin and started humming a little tune under her breath. Memme always hummed when she needed 'spiritual comfort'.

My baby-blanket bundle was glued to my hand. I could see boys and girls behind their mothers.

Suddenly, a big woman stepped out of the group. She had her sleeves rolled up to the elbow. Without a word she hoisted our UNRRA quilt bundle off the jeep and flung it over her shoulder. 'Here, let me help,' she said in Estonian. 'You've probably come a long way and are tired. My name is Lepatree.' And Mrs Lepatree carried the first and biggest of our bundles into the house.

As if on cue, arms reached out for other bundles, and soon everybody was helping us to move in. A woman came and asked my name, but I was unable to speak. I was so surprised to find myself among Estonians. I had forgotten there were other Estonians in the world after spending nearly a year among Germans. I now spoke German fluently.

We were shown to our room.

'This is our room?' asked my mother, raising her voice. It was the size of a large closet. And there were four of us, counting Unki, who had still to arrive.

An argument began between Mimma and the house superintendent. It ended with both of them and the driver getting into the jeep and driving off – to the 'office'. Memme and I were left on our bundles, which were sticking halfway out into the hall, so that we could not close the door.

'All right,' said Memme firmly. 'Let's get to work.'

She removed her jacket and banged her hat against the wall. It released a cloud of dust. Then she put it back on again. Memme did not like to be seen without her hat. She said a lady always keeps her hat on in the company of strangers. She handed me a pair of scissors from her handbag and told me to start on the pink bundle first, and to be careful not to cut the cloth. Meanwhile, she worked on the quilt bundle, undoing the stitches that held it together.

I could not concentrate with all those people watching us, standing around in the open doorway. Now and then someone popped a head inside to ask if we needed help – and took a long look at our things at the same time. Memme started humming again.

I would have hummed too, only I couldn't follow a tune. When it was time for singing I found the way out of trouble was to keep silent. I'd just open my mouth and pretend. But it was impossible to pretend humming, except in my mind. So I hummed in my mind.

And then I cut into the blanket.

While all the people had been looking at us, I had peeped back too, politely, of course, and had noticed that all the girls were wearing identical dresses. Not thick woollen ones like mine, patched and darned, but thin summer dresses with tiny white flowers on a blue background. And most of the children were barefoot.

It had happened again! Only this time it was even worse. The dress was like a uniform. In Hausberge, at least, there had been variations. Sometimes instead of a dirndl dress, it was all right just to wear a gathered skirt with a ribbon border. But one had to have a frilly blouse and white knee socks.

I had had none of those things when we arrived in Germany, and because most Germans wore 'national costume', I had stuck out like a sore thumb. Just as I would in this camp.

I shook Memme's sleeve urgently and whispered that I had to have a dress like that and I must be allowed to go barefoot. But Memme would not hear of it. She was in no mood to discuss the dress. 'Go out and play,' she said.

Never! It was impossible!

A nightmare was starting again, and I decided that the best way out of it was to stay inside the house and in our room and never to go out again as long as I lived – or at least until I got the dress. I also hoped they might start bombing again! I had got my own back on my former teacher, Mr Koch, by wishing the Americans would bomb the schoolhouse. Every time the planes flew over I used to wish it. Bomb the schoolhouse, bomb the schoolhouse! I crossed my fingers and hoped to die, until one night a bomb hit the schoolhouse. It went smack into the middle of it, and the whole cliff went down with the schoolhouse, into the river Weser. No more Mr Koch. No more school! But then I started to feel guilty. No one knew my wishes were that powerful! Even Memme didn't know it had been my doing, and she says, 'Lies have short legs, same as guilt and deception.' It was just as well we had left Hausberge!

'What are you doing?' asked Memme suspiciously.

'Wishing,' I said.

As nothing exciting happened, the people soon tired of watching us and returned to their rooms. A good smell of cooking began to fill the hall. I was hungry.

It was starting to get dark outside. The lamps were lighted in the hall and on the landing. All the doors led off the hall. There was no light in our room, just an empty light socket.

I sat down in the doorway, as I usually did when I was waiting for someone. I hoped Mimma would not be long, and that Unki would find us without difficulty. There was a possibility that either of them could get me a dress 'underhand', as they managed to get sugar and flour, sewing needles, and salt.

Although the hall was empty, I could hear people talking in their rooms. Dishes clattered. Once in a while, a door would open and someone would come into the kitchen with a covered dish or to get a pan, or to fill a bucket at the kitchen pump. The pump was worked continually, and there were other women in the kitchen whom I hadn't seen yet, frying and talking. It was so strange to hear Estonian and to be able to understand snatches of their conversation that I almost expected to see Tätä appear out of nowhere with a bucket, followed by a black cat, or to see my father darkening the doorway with his tall shadow.

I hugged my knees and rested my chin on them. It was almost bedtime. In Hausberge I had often fallen asleep on the stairs. Because of the air raids, I was terrified of the attic and felt the bottom step was closest to the cellar. The attic had been the centre of my nightmares. But we lived in the attic, so as soon as I was asleep, Unki would carry me to bed. I wished we could have lived in the cellar or right in the air-raid shelter. But this night, there was no cellar or attic to worry about, just the nightmares that I started to dread already. And I dreaded going to sleep.

Memme let me talk about my nightmares when she wasn't busy. But now she was hunting for candles. The small window let in very little light and, as it got darker, no light at all. An apple-tree branch was brushing the glass from outside, going tap, tap, tap, with the wind.

But it was a summer wind. It cooled me through the big open door and dusted me off after the hot day. I longed to take off my thick wool dress and thick stockings, but Memme hadn't said I could yet.

She had found a candle. As soon as she had lighted it she noticed the big cut I had made in the blanket, but didn't comment. The pink bundle kept our silver. Sugar tongs of

'Russian silver' and a couple of teaspoons were all that was left. The rest had 'paid our passage'.

Memme placed the candle on the windowsill. The flame flickered and was pulled in all directions by unseen fingers. I thought of a game to play with the shadows on the wall. A gruesome giant was bending over our bundles, arranging them into a corner. It was filling sacks with straw, 'for us to sleep on until we get beds,' said the giant in Memme's voice. It was a nice giant and handed me some bread, ordinary rye bread, for my supper.

Munching the crust, which had turned hard, I continued my vigil. A new moon was rising behind the church steeple. I had a clear view across the yard. I crossed my fingers and wished 'If you're not too busy, Jesus, please let me have a blue dress like the one all the other girls are wearing. It's UNRRA issue. So if you know UNRRA, maybe he'll let you have one, seeing you are who you are. Thank you!' To which I hastily added 'Amen!' That way it was both a wish and a prayer.

When I opened my eyes, the moon had gone behind a cloud. A bad omen, Mimma would have said. Memme was more on the religious side, but Mother was definitely superstitious. I wondered if it was worse to be 'damned' or to put shoes on the table with the toes pointing inward.

The women in the kitchen had finished their talking and cooking. The pump was silent. They all went into their rooms, and I guessed everybody was eating supper now, the whole world over. Unki had taught me about 'the whole world over' as we lay on our backs in the grass, staring into a starry sky, watching it move and pretending we were lying on the side of a tennis ball that was going around and around slowly.

It was dark on the stairs, but I noticed a sudden movement. A girl was sitting there, half hidden by the banister. She was clutching a doll and sucking her thumb – and staring down at me.

I stared back just as rudely. We stayed that way for a long time, barely able to see each other in the dark.

Finally she stood up and started down slowly, one step at a time. I saw she was wearing 'the dress'.

'What do you want?' I asked in German.

'Nothing,' she replied in Estonian.

I showed her our window, how small it was.

'That's nothing! Ours is even smaller.' She said I could come up and have a look.

I paused, wary of trickery. But then I remembered how much I had wanted to have friends my own age, and this girl wasn't laughing at me.

We were just going when a door opened on the landing, and a woman came to the top of the stairs. 'My mother,' said the girl, and froze. It was Mrs Lapatree.

'Monika!' her mother called impatiently. 'Come up here at once!'

The girl hesitated, then ran upstairs quickly, without a backward glance. Their door banged shut. Our candle went out.

But my heart was beating wildly. I had talked to an Estonian girl my own age, and it had been a friendly contact. The only other girl friend I had ever had was in Haapsalu, a girl called Viive Kotipuu. Her mother was a friend of my mother, and we often had been forced to play together just because the mothers were visiting. She was a clever pants because she had a toy post office and a real pony. They had an aunt living with them. Her father had been deported to Siberia during the first Russian occupation. We quarrelled a lot, but at other times, we played 'nicely'. They left Estonia about the same time we did.

My eyes were starting to get heavy when Mother and the superintendent came back from the office. They seemed to have settled their differences and were talking 'theatre'. He was saying how he had seen all Mimma's plays and was describing each scene in detail. I saw Mother stifle a yawn and saw her discreetly look at her watch. She began taking the combs out of her hair when he wasn't looking.

Finally, they said good night.

'And we'll get you a bigger room as soon as one becomes available,' he promised.

'That's fine,' said Mother, and stumbled over me in the dark. She seemed preoccupied. Maybe she had hoped to meet my father here at this camp. He had promised to join us 'later'. Two years seemed late enough.

'Paul here yet?' she asked Memme, meaning Unki.

Memme shook her head.

Mother began to undress, and Memme motioned for me to do likewise. It was still a novelty to undress at night and wear a nightgown, actually one of Memme's old summer dresses. And it was a relief to get out of my woollen stockings and wriggle my toes.

My mattress was under the table. The freshly stuffed straw rustled and bit through the sheets. Memme was sighing and turning also, and Mother kept getting up. 'I can't imagine where Paul's got to,' she kept saying, looking at her watch in the moonlight. 'It's half past one!'

Unki was supposed to 'catch a lift with a friend'. I loved Unki very much. He had found us in Hausberge about the time the schoolhouse was bombed and had tried to protect me from the other kids, to whom I was still a foreigner, by taking me with him whenever he could. We collected firewood together. We sneaked into orchards and stole peaches or cherries or could be found lying down in the middle of a lima-bean field, eating lima beans and studying the 'constellations' before it got completely dark and we had to hurry home before the air raids came.

I knew that if Unki didn't come soon ... and then I heard singing. It came staggered and uneven up the silent midnight road. Three voices, but I knew Unki's right away.

Unki had caught up with us. He had found the camp right away, but on the road to Number Nine he, too, had passed by the brewery, and found it a good place to stop for a quick snort.

Closer and closer the singers came, followed by raucous laughter and another song, this time in Estonian.

'Mari's white knickers are a sight to behold . . .'

Then Unki sang alone, the *Marseillaise*. Unki was fresh from the French Foreign Legion and very proud of it.

Mimma's mattress became strangely quiet. Memme sat up. Angry voices were roused behind the wall. A door slammed. The hall light went on. My heart stopped beating.

Dogs had started barking all over the camp now. Windows were opened, but the singers paid no heed. They had stopped by our gate. 'Mari's white knickers,' rang out again. The second verse.

Mother jumped up, grabbed her coat, and left.

Memme had stopped moving and was listening, as I was. We heard words like 'decent people' and 'bloody drunks' and 'We don't care whose brother you are!'

But the singing did stop abruptly, on a half-note. Mother was explaining to the superintendent, who said, 'Is that so?' as if he didn't believe a word of it.

Eventually the commotion ceased. The hall light went off again, and people returned to their rooms, still muttering.

Mother threw her coat aside and, without another word, climbed back into bed. Unki sat down on his mattress and stayed sitting, head in his hands. He didn't even take his coat off.

I could see him clearly in the shaft of moonlight through the little window but dared not go to him yet. So I held my breath some more. It made me hot all over and my heart seemed to be beating in my stomach. When my mother was cross, I didn't think of her as being Mimma but as someone else's mother, somebody I didn't really know.

Memme was tossing and turning. Mother also couldn't get comfortable.

A long time later, I saw Unki lie down, but not to sleep. He was staring at the ceiling.

Dear Unki! I wanted so much to go and take his hand. The loud arrival was nothing new. It had been worse the night he arrived in Hausberge, just back from Indochina. But the stories he told me, each one more exciting than the last! About jungles, snakes, and crocodiles. How he had wrestled with a lion once. About deserts and riding on camels. And about coffee mountains in Brazil. And finally how he had walked three hundred kilometres through the Russian lines, backwards, looking for us. He had walked backwards because every time he met a Russian division on the road, he'd tell them he was Russian. 'Going home,' he'd shout, waving a red handkerchief he kept specially for that purpose. He spoke fluent Russian. And sometimes he even let them give him a ride up the road. But as soon as they dropped him he would be off the other way again. And that's how he found us in that attic in Hausberge. Or, rightly, we found him, during an air raid, drowning out the sound of the bombs with his singing.

'My God! That's Paul!' Mimma said, and went white as a sheet.

Now I wanted to take his hand and comfort him, as he had often comforted me. I knew he felt bad. He always felt bad after a 'scene' and most times walked away to be alone.

At last Memme started to snore, softly, bubblingly. Then Mimma's mattress became still.

Unki had been waiting for the same moment. He sat up, put away his coat, and began to unwind his feet. He only had one pair of socks and wore rags, which were just as good, wound around and around.

When Unki began to rub his corns, I knew the time was right. I slipped off my hay sack, quiet as a mouse, and took his hand.

'I'm glad you are here,' I whispered happily. 'I was waiting for you.'

Unki's gold teeth flashed in the moonlight. And he hugged me close.

7 The Dress

It was too bad about the dress. Memme said she couldn't help me. Mother explained that camp clothes were issued by UNRRA and that the relief association gave us things. We couldn't ask for them. She said I was making a big thing out of nothing. Memme thought so too, but neither of them had been able to protect me against Lisa or Mr Koch. There were some things that grown-ups could not understand or even see with their own eyes. This was one of them.

Mimma was the first to get up in the morning – she always did when she stayed with us, which wasn't very often. She usually left while it was still dark with an empty rucksack and said she'd be back in a few days. When she returned a few days later, her rucksack was always bulging with potatoes, onions, carrots, apples, and cabbages. Sometimes she'd have tins of sardines in her pockets or bags of flour hanging around her neck on string, and sometimes she had a squashed paper bag of berries – for me. I guessed she foraged around like Unki and I used to, in burned-out warehouses and on abandoned farms. She was always completely exhausted when she came back and immediately collapsed on the bed, where she would sleep for a day and a night.

Unki went out in the mornings too, but he never went far, nor did he stay long. He usually returned with a grin and at least three fresh eggs tucked in his coat pocket, and sometimes with a dead chicken stuffed into his knapsack, feathers and all.

Memme always cooked everything for us, but kept the eggs

for a cake, if there was a birthday coming, just as mine would be coming soon.

The day after we arrived in the camp, Mimma and Unki went out early. Memme got up too and went straight into the kitchen. She had to share it with the other women, and as we had no pots or pans at all, except an enamel coffee pot, she had to wait a long time for her turn. I tried to stay as close to her as possible.

Time went by slowly. It hardly seemed to move at all.

When I didn't follow Memme, I stayed in our room and hid behind the bit of curtain she had tacked up for decency, our room being on ground level.

There was no time lag out there on the road. I watched several of the girls from our house playing hopscotch with what must have been German girls because they all spoke German. They were all wearing the dress, of course, and strange-looking wooden clogs with canvas uppers, if they weren't barefoot.

To the right of the house and across the road was a big meadow with a giant swing tied to the branches of an ancient oak. Not a minute passed all day when the swing was empty. The younger children used it in the morning and the older kids as soon as school was out. It was only a few days to summer recess. I wouldn't have to go to school until next term – a chilling thought! – unless there was an earthquake or a tidal wave.

That girl Monika was out there too, talking loudly in German. It seemed that the German kids lived in the house next to ours, on the other side of a drainage ditch. They were called Anu and Maret and Sigrid. 'It's your turn, Sigrid. Come on!' And 'You're out!' Anu appeared to be Estonian, but it was hard to tell, since they all wore the same dresses.

When someone looked towards the house, I ducked out of sight, afraid to be seen, though they must have known I was watching.

One day I noticed that the girl Maret Ramins wasn't wearing

the dress but just an ordinary cotton one. It was very much like a summer dress I had, but which I wasn't allowed to wear until summer. Memme's summer started exactly on the first day of July – not one day sooner.

It was an interesting observation, and I found out the girl's name was Ramins because her mother called her from an upstairs window. 'Maret Ramins!' she called sharply. The rest I didn't understand. But I had seen an alternative to the blue dress, and I knew it was only a few more days till summer.

Monika appeared at our door a little later, smiling. I had started to hate her a little because of the dress and because she could have come and played with me instead of going to the others. She was the only one who had approached me at all. And then she had let me down.

'My name is Monika,' she said pleasantly, as if the past week hadn't existed. And she looked around the doorway into our room again without leave. She had her doll with her.

'I know!' I said.

'Come and play with me.'

Her quick eyes noticed our potty while she was talking. It was peeping out from under the chair. As potties go, I thought it was a pretty nice one. But drats! It had to be half full! Memme hadn't had time to empty it yet. There was a farm toilet between the pigsty and the kitchen, just an enclosed hole in the ground with a wooden bench over it. The bench had a hole in the middle, but it was so big that once I almost fell through into the septic tank, so I hardly ever used it. I was afraid of it.

'Where do you want to play?' I asked. I was not going out of the house.

'Out there.' She pointed to the yard. 'I know a good place.'

'I'm not playing with any Germans,' I told Monika outright.

'There are no Germans here.' She seemed surprised.

'But I heard you all talking in German.'

'Well?'

'So I'm not playing with Germans, and that's that!' I insisted.

Monika put her thumb into her mouth as if she didn't know what I was talking about. She wanted to play dolls. I didn't have one. The only one doll I had been allowed to bring from Estonia I decided to leave nameless. She had become sick in the head. I had dropped her one night on the way to an air-raid shelter. People were running past us and somebody stepped on her head. Memme pasted some of her own hair over the dent, but it still didn't look right. So I bandaged her up. She was dying. But she was still a good soldier. Unki thought she might pull through. I hadn't decided yet, one way or the other.

'I don't care about dolls anyway,' I said suddenly. 'And I don't want to play with you.'

Monika looked surprised, but not for long. 'Bet you don't want to play because your doll can't go wee-wee! And who wants to play with you anyway! Dressed like a clown, with your stockings hanging down!' She whirled on her heel and went outside to join the others.

The rat! I watched her go on alone to the swing, dragging her doll through the long grass. How I wished I'd had the courage to go with her! I bet the grass would reach my ankles.

When Memme came in from the kitchen I asked her if I could wear my green summer dress yet. It really was warm outside. But Memme shook her head. 'Not yet. The ground is still frozen.'

Other people's summer just wasn't Memme's summer!

There were still five days to go. How long would it take for the ground to defrost? I wondered. It looked fine already, especially out there in the meadow by the swing. Everybody was shrieking with joy. And they were all barefoot and half naked!

Two boys from the house across the ditch came around the corner carrying a bucket. They stopped directly under our window. I ducked out of sight, but I could hear them talking.

From the sound of the spade, they were digging for worms. I had seen those two earlier, fishing from a bridge that spanned a pond on the edge of the meadow, by the schoolhouse.

Crouching on Memme's red-knitted blanket bundle, I strained my ears for what they were talking about. But I couldn't understand a word of it. And then I realized, they weren't talking in German, or in Estonian. One boy was called Vilis and he was Maret's brother.

'Memme, Memme, who lives across the yard?'

'In Number Eleven?'

'Yes, yes!'

'It's the beginning of the Latvian sector.'

Latvians!

'The Lithuanians live across the bridge, beyond the schoolhouse.' Memme sat me down for a bowl of flour gruel. I hated the stuff, but this time it almost tasted good.

'Where do the Germans live?'

'There are no Germans in this camp,' Memme told me. 'Is that why you won't go out?'

'No,' I said quickly. But I thought, Imagine that!

'If you eat all your gruel, I have a surprise for you.' Memme held one hand behind her back.

'Chocolate,' I said at once, although I could barely remember what chocolate tasted like.

'White bread,' said Memme. She handed me a piece of bread that was chalk white, even whiter than cake. But it tasted of nothing. Nothing at all!

'It's better with jam,' said Unki, who had come home at dawn and was sleeping under a cold compress.

I went back to my place at the window, but this time I climbed onto the highest bundle. Peering through the apple-tree branches, I could see far enough down the road to see it make a curve beyond the bridge. Lithuanians!

Of course they would be speaking German. It was the only

common language. Still, I had never met any Latvians or Lithuanians before, and there was still a case for caution.

The only time the swing was empty was late in the evenings, around supper-time. And that evening I decided to take my chances, at a time when no one would notice me.

I waited until the last child had left. The meadow was empty; the swing hung solitary and inviting, yet it was still light enough to see it. The camp was quiet. There was smoke pouring from every chimney. Food smells filled the house. Memme was busy in the kitchen. And although the food smells made me dizzy with expectation, it wasn't enough to change my mind.

I slipped out. It was easy.

In a twinkling I had crossed the road, slid down the grass bank, and started running. I had eyes only for the swing. A deep hollow had been worn into the sand directly underneath the seat. I wondered if I could reach the seat, which was swaying slightly. Was it still moving from the last swinging? Or was it being nudged by the evening breeze? The sunset cast an orange-pink glow over the schoolhouse. Roosters were crowing, and large shadows had already started to patch the ground.

Just a couple of tries was all I wanted – just once up and down. Then I'd come back home and be satisfied until Memme let me out in the green summer dress.

The grass did reach my ankles. I knew it would. It was cool and silky, even through the thick stockings. I imagined myself already swooshing up into the sky, the wind in my ears, my stomach all tight and tickly. And that sudden *ugh!* of the downward plunge. It was a feeling like when my father used to throw me in the air and catch me coming down, or like waking up from my nightmares and finding myself in this camp, which was unlike any camp I'd ever heard of.

I was so eager to get there that I didn't look to right or left or up or down. Just ahead. And that's when it happened.

Suddenly, a terrible pain shot through my foot.

It was so awful, I didn't even scream. I sat in the grass and just stared and stared. A nail was sticking out of the sole of my shoe and had gone right into my foot. It was crusty with rust and had a sort of flat disk instead of a head. When I pressed my foot, I didn't feel anything. It was only when I let go and saw the blood that the pain started.

Screaming, limping, jumping, hopping, and crawling, I started back for the house.

I hadn't reached the road yet, when it looked as though the whole camp was running towards me. Latvians from Number Eleven, Lithuanians from across the bridge, and Estonians from Number Nine and Number Ten.

Memme was in front with Mrs Lepatree. Both had their aprons on and Memme's arms were white with flour.

'She must be taken to the doctor at once,' said Memme.

Unki wasn't home. Mimma was away too. So it was the house superintendent who lifted me onto his shoulders and carried me to the camp doctor. Into the Lithuanian sector we went, past the schoolhouse and the church. A lot of people came with us, mainly children, and when I saw them, I screamed as loudly as I could. I was sure no one had ever had such a big rusty nail go through the foot! Or suffered such pain! As I screamed louder, their eyes filled with awe, fear, and admiration. There were Anu and the two Latvian girls, Maret and Sigrid. And Maret's brother Vilis. They thought I was dying.

The doctor said it wasn't too bad. He reached into his bag for a sharp, wicked-looking knife. I knew it! He was going to cut my foot off.

'This won't hurt,' said the doctor, in that sly way that meant it would. He blinked his eyes at Memme and kept the knife just out of sight. So I screamed louder still. No one was going to cut my foot off!

'Now look here,' said the doctor.

The superintendent was called in, to help hold me down.

It was all finished for me, and Memme wasn't much help. Wringing her flour-coated hands, she pleaded for me to be quiet, to let the 'good doctor' cut my foot off. And then she remembered she had left our supper on the stove. No supper and no foot! And the doctor was losing his patience. He made a few quick moves. The nail was out.

When the wound was clean and bandaged, I still had my foot. I demanded to be reassured, and the doctor then uncovered my toes and counted them for me. 'All right?' he asked.

Slightly shamefaced, I let the superintendent carry me back through the outer office, where everybody looked at me as though they must have heard my screams. I couldn't walk, of course, and was carried back to Number Nine, again on the superintendent's shoulders.

After that night, everything changed. The next morning Mrs Lepatree came to our door to ask how I felt. Was my foot still painful? Was there anything I needed?

Vilis and Maret came and stood in the hall, while Memme talked to their mother in German. Unki came home and carried me out to the garden to sit in the sun on his grey soldier blanket. As my foot was heavily bandaged, I couldn't wear stockings. The wool dress had been stained with blood. I had to wear the green cotton one. There I was, in a cotton dress and barefoot, and it was only the twenty-sixth of June!

I had never known life could be like this. The kids clamoured around me, asking if my foot still hurt. 'Of course,' I said.

'Was there a lot of blood?' asked one who had missed the actual scene.

'At least ten pints,' I said.

Vilis' friend, whose name was Uno, said he had seen the nail come right out the other side of my foot. 'It was at least six inches long,' he described it.

Was it really? I didn't remember it being that long, but if he said so, it must have been. 'At least six inches,' I agreed.

I felt like a princess out of a fairy tale. With each telling the nail got longer and longer, and there was more and more blood. I had never been so happy. Not since . . . a long time ago!

The next day was the same. I was carried back into the garden. A game of hunt the potato started around me. The potato was hidden under my blanket. Memme sat with some other women in the shade of the apple tree, beating eggs, making 'goggle-moggle' for me as a special treat. Eggs beaten fluffy with sugar.

Mrs Lepatree brought me a cup of red-currant juice sweetened with honey. All that and more! I lay back dizzy with the unaccustomed special treatment and the wonder of being smiled at by strangers, of being liked and being part of a group. As for the kids – I had become one of 'them', and now it was 'us'. I hoped my foot would never heal.

Anu, who *was* Estonian and lived in Number Ten, lent me her special picture book about Estonian shot-putters. It had been her father's, who had also become 'lost' during the war. I treasured it appropriately, though I couldn't understand it. She lent it in case I 'got bored'.

But I would never get bored now! Even when the games moved farther down the garden, I was still included by a shout or a glance as the ball bounced my way or landed on my blanket.

And then the most surprising thing happened! Monika, whom I had almost forgotten, came and sat down on my blanket. She was in a bad mood. She said she wished she had a green summer dress like mine, instead of always the same old blue one!

As my foot started healing, I was able to leave the blanket and hobble around. Anu, Maret, Sigrid, and I played hide and seek, and they gave me extra time to hide. I learned a new German counting rhyme:

Ich und Du, bunte Kuh,
Müller's Esel, das bist Du.

Roughly translated, it meant, 'Me and you, a cow of brilliant hue, the miller's donkey, that is you!'

Out with the first light and just so busy, I barely had time to eat. I still wanted the blue dress because everybody else had one, but it wasn't so important anymore. Maret said she had waited two months to get one. The girls talked a lot about clothes – and the women too, I noticed, as I began to feel at home and moved about more.

I noticed the boys hardly cared what they wore, which seemed the best way to be. There was so much time wasted on clothes talk, and it was a subject I was trying to forget. The time could have been put to better use. It was very frustrating. But I didn't want to be disloyal to the first real friends I'd ever had, Anu and Maret.

When we were at the swing, and I loved swinging, I couldn't help but wish we could join the boys down at the pond, fishing for frogs. But when I mentioned it to Maret, she said 'Yuk'. Anu said her mother would beat her if she so much as went near the pond.

I'd heard there was an open grave in the cemetery.

'How awful,' they said, and looked at me strangely.

So I didn't say anymore. It was wonderful enough just the way it was. I didn't want to be ungrateful. Still . . .

One day, while I was playing hopscotch on my good leg with Anu, Maret, and Sigrid, and having lots of fun, Mimma came from the office and told me we were moving. To house Number Fifteen. To a bigger room.

I had completely forgotten about our needing a bigger room! I looked at her in dismay. 'Now?'

'Now,' she said, clapping her hands briskly.

Memme must have known ahead of time, because she was already pinning her hat on when I entered the room. 'Memme,' I pleaded desperately, but I knew that things like 'moving' and 'going on ahead' were out of her hands. She said I should be happy, we were getting a big room, big enough for all of us. And we could shut the door.

But Maret Ramins sneaked up beside me and whispered that house Number Fifteen was at the other side of the camp, on the German boundary. I remembered seeing it when we first arrived. It was down the right fork from Number One. It seemed like miles away and with nothing but fields in between.

Maret nodded and continued. 'There was trouble at Number Fifteen only two weeks ago.' And she told me how there was a German farm right across the yard from it and how the Germans came at night to tear up the vegetable gardens. She said she wouldn't want to live there, and stepped away from me, as though I had already left or were a part of that trouble.

A camp official came to show us the way. He piled our bundles onto a pushcart, which he and Unki pushed between them, and suggested a shortcut across the fields, along a field path, rather than going the long way around.

We crossed the ditch and headed for the fields by a deeply rutted path that was overgrown and showed little use.

Mimma walked in front, carrying her high heels. The cart rumbled and bounced. The men talked and sweated in the hot sun. Unki tied his handkerchief at its four corners and wore it to protect his bald head. Unki had never had any hair on his head and had two baby pictures to prove it.

Memme and I trudged along behind, Memme carrying a bowl of curds covered by a cloth. She found it hard walking in the deep ruts. The almost ripe wheat and rye rippled on either side of us, buzzing with insects and dotted with poppies and cornflowers. It was so hot that the air wavered. Everything was blurred for me anyway, as hot tears forced themselves across my vision. But there was nothing I could do about it. I kept looking back until house Number Nine disappeared completely behind the wheat, along with Maret, Anu, and Sigrid, and the rest of my newfound friends. And I bet the swing was still swinging. I bet there were boys fishing in the reeds, and I bet Maret and Anu had continued their hopscotch without me, just as if I had never been there.

The last time I looked back, I couldn't even see the church spire.

And last of all, I had never got the dress!

8 A Room and a Half

The most surprising thing about House Number Fifteen was that it was identical to Number Nine. The same carriage entrance, the same layout of rooms, and there was even a pigsty in the same place. Only this one contained pigs. There were three pigs. The Angoroffs' pig, the Petersons' pig, and the Mölders' pig.

But no kids. Not a single one.

Our 'bigger room' turned out to be a room and a half. When Memme was searching for a good place to put my bed so the bugs wouldn't find me right away, she moved the table from the wall. Suddenly she noticed an uneven line in the wallpaper. It appeared to have been cut through with a knife. Mimma bent to investigate and found the door to a secret chamber. There was just a small trapdoor with steps leading down to a tiny room. Even the window was masked from the outside by a curtain of ivy.

I said I wanted it to be my room, but Unki got it. Memme said that a man needs a place 'to throw his coat'. And Unki's coat was huge.

I had barely put my bundle down before I was warned off the German property next door. A narrow dirt road separated the German yard from ours. The farmer had erected a chain-link fence with barbed wire along the top and planted shrubbery to screen his greenhouses and keep us out. And as soon as we turned into the path, the farmer's dogs started barking, two huge Alsatians, which were kept at bay by the fence. They were obviously guard dogs.

The road led onto the farmer's fields, but it did not look at all abandoned, like the cart path we had come along. It curved out of sight towards a distant wood. Right away it caught my eye, though one had to pass the farm to use it.

Farm noises were everywhere, a strange contrast to the silent farmyards in the camp. The farmer had a wagon and harness in the entrance yard. Chickens strayed across the road. Pigs were grunting, cows mooed. There was a pungent smell of animals and manure and constant activity. The farmer and his wife (who wore the green-and-black velvet folk costume), were loading a cart of turnips, helped by their three teenage sons. They were lifting sacks, shouting at the horses, and going about their business, but after two years of experience in German villages, I knew it was the boys I had to look out for.

'Keep away from there,' said the house superintendent, who nodded to them in greeting, while showing us around. I heard him say he hadn't known there was to be a child, meaning me. He didn't seem very pleased about it.

As soon as the tour was over, the unpacking done, and the newness of moving into a strange room had dulled, I was back sitting in the doorway, just as if we had just moved into the camp.

I watched the Germans finish loading their turnips and watched the cart rumble away with one of the sons at the reins, a big blond boy of about nineteen, apparently the oldest son. The rest of the family went into the house to wash.

What now? I wondered.

I had wanted to explore the woods, but Memme said it was out of the question. And I wasn't even sure I would have dared go so far. I didn't want to stay inside our room, either. There was nothing to do outside! Nothing to do inside!

I climbed onto a covered well at the side of the house and pretended I was king of the mountain. But it was no fun being king of anything if there were no lesser kings or lowly subjects looking on from below. And to think that on arrival at this camp, I had actually wished there wouldn't be any children!

It was back to playing with Memme, as we had played all through the war. But she was much busier than she had been before.

Mimma too was very busy. She had a new job with the camp administration. She rushed around in jeeps, laughed a lot, and spoke English. She carried important papers and flicked cigarette butts into the air; then rr-umm-rr-umm, she drove off again in a cloud of dust. I wished she would take me with her, but she said she couldn't. She kissed me and embraced me on coming and going. 'Hello!' and 'Good-bye!' But at least she was living in the same room with us. She had always gone 'ahead', to look for work and so we had never had a chance actually to live together. It was good to see her, and I waited for her to return every day from work.

The rest of the time I was with Memme, or when Memme went off to Stadthagen, the nearest town, to sell Camels at the station, I went into the pigsty to scratch the Angoroffs' pig's tummy with the kitchen broom. He was the fattest and ugliest pig of all, but he loved it when I scratched his hide. He rolled over and grunted with pleasure.

Unki was 'working out a new route' and was also away most of the day. Now that Mother worked at the office, it was up to him to supply most of our food, to supplement the rations.

'Can I go back to Number Nine to play?' I asked Memme one day, as she was leaving. 'I would only stay an hour. I would be back for supper.'

Memme said it was too far.

So I climbed to the top of a huge pear tree in front of the house, and watched her disappear out of sight. I could see Stadthagen from up there. And I could also see the village, part of the schoolhouse roof, and most of the church spire. I made myself a secret nest at the top of that pear tree. It became my lookout tower. But none of those things solved the problem of having no friends.

The experience of friendships as in Number Nine had been like a dream, a beautiful dream, and I couldn't forget it. A gate had been opened and closed, but it had shown me another world, a world that was safe and wonderful and only a mile or two away. It had nothing to do with the German farm next door or the three German youths or even Germany itself, which was still all around us.

And then I had my ninth birthday.

Birthdays were always special for all of us, even for Mother and Unki. And Memme made them twice as special. Like our Christmases, birthdays, too, had a special ritual. In Estonia, Memme had twined wild strawberry vines around my chair, because my birthday was at strawberry time. For Mimma it was oak leaves or juniper, and for Memme herself, trails of ivy. For Unki, last year, we had brought in birch twigs, which were used in the sauna. 'To cleanse his soul,' said Memme. Unki had missed his sauna and was glad there was one here in the camp.

I could never fall asleep the night before my birthday, but was always waking up and thinking it must be morning. Then, when I knew it was morning, I pretended to be fast asleep.

First came the sounds: rustling paper, tearing noises, and the tying of string. The scissors squeaked and needed oiling. The rattle of the matchbox. Clattering cups and spoons. Whispering, as Mimma got up to take the coffeepot downstairs to the kitchen to be heated. And the smell of roasted coffee and an excited conversation as to where it came from and how it had been acquired.

More whispering when Mimma came back, followed by quiet, very quiet laughter! I heard Unki scratching himself in his room.

At last Memme was ready. I could tell by the smell of candle wax, after the match had been struck. I noted that Memme had been a long time wrapping something.

And then they came to my bed. The smell of candle wax was strong. Lights flickered.

'Wake up, birthday girl!' Memme whispered.

'Happy birthday!' said Mimma, who was holding the cake. It was like a crown of glory in her hand.

And with great yawning and stretching, I pretended to wake up, as if I had slept a whole year.

Mimma put the cake on my bed and I blew out the candles. And of course I had to make a wish, though I didn't expect the door to open suddenly, and myself ... all of us ... to be scooped up by my father and whisked back to Haapsalu. Wishes were like secrets, or magic, or 'nature'. There was no knowing what could come about, or how it might happen.

Mimma went to get the coffeepot.

Unki climbed out of his chamber, a bit late. He was sleepy-eyed and unshaven, and couldn't find his other boot.

I jumped out of bed and hurried to the table. Memme carried the cake ahead of me. Unki sat beside me, still yawning and scratching around in his undershirt. I too had noticed the bed-bugs. There were millions of them. And they all came out at night to bite us.

Unki kissed me and rumpled my hair. He was smiling too. But I knew he had a hangover.

Mimma poured the coffee. Memme cut the cake. 'The recipe calls for six eggs, but it tastes all right,' she said, popping a piece into her mouth. Her eyes were shiny when she looked at me.

Mimma allowed me half a cup of coffee.

And then it was time for the presents. There were three parcels. The biggest one was a doll, from Mimma. I remembered it the moment I saw it. It was from Estonia. It had been Mimma's, the one I had never been allowed to touch.

I looked at the delicate china face, the fine hair and eyelashes. The eyes still opened and closed. Once I had been smacked for trying to see how the eyes worked and now, two years later, it was mine. I placed Marie carefully next to the cake and turned to the smallest parcel. It was from Unki. His penknife, I hoped. But it wasn't. It was just an ordinary penknife with only two blades. Ah, well. It was better than no knife at all!

I thanked Unki and Mimma and turned to the third parcel. It was soft and mysterious, flat and square. I tore off the paper and my heart froze. It was *the dress*, from Memme.

I put the dress on right away and rushed into the yard to show it off, but then I remembered. There was no one to show it off to. Here no one cared what I was wearing.

I sat down sadly on the edge of the well. Wishes were really funny. A wish in one place, if it didn't come true soon enough, could really mess you up somewhere else, or turn out to be completely wrong. One had to be really careful about what one wished for. I had wished there wouldn't be any children in this camp. And here I was alone with my wish in Number Fifteen. I had even forgotten I had wished it. Maybe there was some way to cancel a wish. As for the dress, it was nice but not important anymore. What a letdown! Only the nail in my foot had been important. I would never have known to wish for that!

9 The First House Gang

Unki was building Memme a stove. He had found an old one in the woods and was mounting it on bricks and smashing a hole through the wall of our room for the stovepipe.

Memme and I collected all the old tin cans we could find or salvage from the garbage heap. Memme scoured them out and Unki beat them into shape to make kitchen utensils. And we were really lucky when we found a tin with the lid still partly attached. The lid was bent and padded to make a handle for the 'saucepan'. Memme didn't like to have to share the kitchen and looked forward to cooking on her own stove in her own time without having to wait for her turn.

From my nest in the pear tree, I got a pretty good view of our surroundings – not only the German farm, where I could see into the kitchen window as well as over the hedge, but into the yard of Number Sixteen as well. I observed the goings-on and jotted them down into my code book, which didn't turn out too interesting. There was a child in Number Sixteen, but she never came out and I found out she wasn't well.

But something did happen, which I made a note of and which made me wish I had a pair of binoculars, like the ones most soldiers had. I noticed a bunch of kids around House Number One, kids who always hung around together, like a gang. And I climbed up to my nest mostly to spy on them.

Even from that distance I found out they seemed to like to do the kind of things I wished I could do too, like hanging on to the back of the food truck on Thursdays. I also noted down that they liked to fish. They carried long homemade fishing rods and obviously knew where there was a pond or a river to fish in. Maybe they used the village pond. Once they must have caught a rabbit or something that was wriggling in a bag.

There were five of them, and one was a girl. Not a Maret type of girl-girl who only cared about her dresses, but a boy-type girl, dressed in a pair of boy's pants and a long shirt. The only way I knew she was a girl was by her pigtails. I wondered if she had anyone to comb her hair. It didn't look like it.

I wanted to join the Gang! But first they had to know I existed, and the only way to do that was to keep an eye open for them and then try to meet them on the road or let them see me somewhere else. I could try to meet Unki coming from the brewery, or be casually passing by with that as an excuse, without actually going there. Memme said I must not.

It was like planning a campaign and needed 'correct' discipline and camouflage and black sewing thread as well as the bobbins. To make the binoculars. Memme wagged a warning finger at me to bring it all back. I said I would. I figured it to be a short battle, like just holding a bridge and then finding out that the enemy was an ally after all.

And so it began. I tried the road trick but it didn't work. They saw me and ignored me. Maybe I had been too far away. So I went closer and put my tongue out at them. I wished then I could wiggle my ears like Unki could. And then I ran back quickly into hiding. But they didn't follow me.

I shouted an insult at them from the top of the tree. I really had to raise my voice to make them hear. They turned around. I hoped they would come to look for me. They didn't.

Once they passed under my tree! I held my breath while they were below and decided to follow them, but by the time I had climbed down, they had disappeared or hidden. If they had hidden, it meant the battle had started. I was sure they had, and went in to tell Memme I had found some new friends.

Several days passed before they passed under my tree again, but this time, I felt they had come that way on purpose. And they seemed to be looking around the yard and into the windows. I learned their names. The leader was called Rein. The girl was his sister Erika. And then there was Vello, who wore thick glasses and had his cap on backwards, and Tõnu, who picked his nose. The smallest was redhead Pügi, a weed. A right mess they were, but I loved them. I loved the way they got dirty. I loved the way they were often wet or drying out with mud or grasses sticking to their clothing. I noticed a tidemark around Rein's neck. He hated washing, I could see that. I hated washing my neck too. And I liked the way they talked. Army talk. 'Yes, Herr Commandant!' And 'What did you think of today's action?' 'Two more advances like that, and we'd have had them running. Too bad the mother came out to call them in for supper. We'll try again tomorrow.'

'Rout them and clobber them,' I wanted to shout from my pear tree, whoever 'they' were! But prudence kept me silent. It just wasn't the right time. Memme says there's a time for everything – for sowing, for planting, and for meeting a bunch of kids. Their rough talk, I knew, was just a game. But in Berlin and Hausberge, such talk had been real. And it was probably real outside the camp too. But this camp was magic. It had a glass wall around it. That's how I saw it. We lived in a glass bubble.

However, inside the glass bubble, things still happened. Like when Memme and Mother started talking in Russian. Whenever they talked Russian together it meant something was going on that I wasn't supposed to know about until it happened.

In the Angoroffs' pigsty, I climbed on the dividing wall between the sties and said what was on my mind. 'Stupid pigs,' I told them. 'I don't even like you, but I come and tickle your tummies and you grunt with pleasure. Nobody likes you. They tickle your tummies and feed you while they are planning to eat you one day soon for their supper and make bacon and smoked ham and pork sausage out of you. And while they call you "Notsu, Notsu" and click their tongue and fondle your ear, they're wondering if you're fat enough yet and what good jelly they can make from that ear and trotters. And if you knew all that, you wouldn't lie down and grunt with pleasure, you'd be trying to escape, that's what!' And I whacked the Mölders' pig with the broom.

It lay down immediately, closed its eyes, and rolled over. 'Grunt,' it said.

'Something is going on,' I confided in them. All those whisperings! 'You wait and see,' I told them.

And sure enough! Mimma announced at the dinner table that she was leaving us again, 'going on ahead', this time to England. She said we would join her eventually, as usual. But despite her smile and confident voice, I knew it wasn't quite like that at all. But I also sensed it was, as she said, 'the only way'. And with that kind of alternative I just held my breath inside.

Mimma hugged me and said, 'These are difficult times.' She took my hand and led me to Unki's chamber. There on Unki's bed was a little black rabbit, black all over except for a pink nose that twitched and wriggled.

'She needs a carrot,' said Memme, and went to fetch one.

'Pick her up,' Mother encouraged me. 'She won't bite.'

Of course she didn't bite. She just looked a bit bewildered and wondered where her next meal was coming from. That was nature.

I named her Muki. She really was a beautiful rabbit, and I thanked my mother for her. I didn't know anything I wanted from my mother more than what I had already. But it was no more than what I had always wanted ... maybe for her to be my sister and stay with us, instead of being a mother who had to keep going away.

Muki finished her first carrot and started going lippity-lippity around the room. I picked her up and stroked her black fur and listened to Mother explaining about England – how she was going as a 'swan', and how all the women going on ahead were to be called 'swans', or actually 'cygnets'. They would be working in English hospitals and factories under some government scheme.

I couldn't imagine what hospitals and factories were, but I pretended I knew exactly. It was no surprise about her becoming a swan, though. She was going to fly away as usual. It hardly mattered whether they called it flying or fleeing, which we were supposed to be doing right now.

Mother left early in the morning, while I was still asleep. I felt her kiss me good-bye. And as soon as she was out the door I rushed to the window and saw her in a truck with a lot of other women, waving, waving to Memme, who was standing in the road blowing her nose.

To be sure Muki wouldn't run away, Unki built her a sturdy cage. Muki went to live with Unki in his secret chamber. We were not supposed to have animals, but the house was full of pigs! I couldn't see how it mattered to have a little rabbit. Still Memme wouldn't let me take Muki outside, not even with a string tied around her leg. I fed her dandelion leaves, fresh grass, dried apples, and carrots, and she was happy. We cleaned the cage every day. I held the pan. Memme sniffed the air and said Unki's room was starting to smell worse than usual.

Muki was a great friend, but she did keep me confined to the house. And I wanted to be outside, keeping track of the First House Gang.

Luckily, Muki didn't mind my leaving her as long as she had plenty of water and a dried apple or carrot to gnaw on.

I made one more attempt to join the Gang. I presented myself at their gate one morning, just as they were coming out. I folded my arms and pretended to be passing the time of day, propped up against the gate post of Number One, just whistling ...

'Who's that girl?' asked Rein, as if he had never seen me before.

'Just a dumb girl,' said Tõnu, curling his lip in contempt. 'Probably lost her dolly. Maybe she wants to play houses or doctor.'

'Yes, let's play doctor!' shouted redhead Pügi with delight. But he became quiet when he saw the others glaring at him.

'We don't want any more girls in this division,' said Rein. 'So run along home to your mother.'

'Girls are stupid,' said Vello, warming to the subject, but Erika cut him short so viciously that I felt it was time to be moving along too.

That girl Erika!

As soon as I had backed away they forgot me and climbed the wall to the brewery. I dared not follow them this time, though I knew Unki wasn't there. I had left him sprawled out on his bed, half on and half off. Memme had covered the top half of him with a blanket and removed his boots.

'Turks!' I called after them, and hoped they would all break their legs. I could do without them. I could find my own secret places and go my own way. I could even do my own fishing – one day, when I was allowed into the village again.

Cat was a great explorer. She kept her tail up high, listening to enemy broadcasts, and was always ready to flush out spies from the bushes – spies disguised as birds and field mice, of course, which was very clever.

And Muki kept a lookout through Unki's window, and reported to me in the evening when I came home to feed her. She had good radar ears and a sensitive nose.

Summer had arrived at last, even in Memme's calendar, and I was out all day, sometimes so early that the dew was still on the grass. It was Cat who woke me up, by biting my nose. 'Get up, you lazy foot soldier,' she purred. 'And let's go!'

Cat and I usually shared a cup of powdered milk for breakfast. If Unki was awake, I was able to get through to Muki and give her the day's instructions. 'Keep a lookout for enemy aircraft.' Then I hurried outdoors.

Cat led the way.

We sneaked past the German farm to the woods. Memme sighed and said it was all right. 'But be careful!'

And sometimes she came to check on me, with a piece of bread wrapped in a cloth or with an apple, as I often forgot to come home for lunch. She brushed the hair from my face and said she was glad. She was glad I was happy. I was certainly busy and sometimes didn't come home until the last glow of the sunset had faded away.

Our assignment was to find out nature's secrets. We lay in the grass waiting to see it grow and tried to catch a flower as it opened. I wanted to see a squirrel have babies, or see an egg open and a baby bird come out. There were plenty of birds' nests around with eggs in them, but somehow all the magic happened at night, and Memme wouldn't let me stay up all night. So I tried to get up early, but I never got there early enough.

Yet, Memme had seen magic. She'd seen the end of the rainbow once when she was a little girl. She had climbed down from her father's wagon and stood in the rainbow, striped with colours. Her father had stayed with the horse, but he had seen it too. And they had told everyone, but nobody had believed them. 'Don't spill the secrets of your heart,' warned Memme, 'or your heart will dry up for the lack of them.'

I wouldn't have told anyone. But still I didn't see a single bumblebee being born, or caterpillar changing into a butterfly, or even a mushroom bursting out of the ground. Yet it happened every day the world over.

A stream ran alongside the secret wood, and I guessed this was where the Gang went fishing. Frogs jumped and rested in the reeds. Dragonflies swooped and hovered delicately over the water. Birds chirped, and squirrels chased each other around and around tree trunks.

Mimma wrote letters from England, and I always took them to the woods with me, to reread them at my own pace. Memme read too fast. I wanted to know what England was like. Did they have houses? Did they have bridges? And what did they look like? I knew Japanese houses were made of paper and their bridges were hump-backed. There was a book about Japan in Memme's bundles, dedicated to Mausi, whoever that was, 'with best wishes'.

Mimma didn't describe anything like that. She just said she was working, and that she was thinking of us. She sent her love and kisses at the end of each letter. I wished she would send them on something more solid. Paper lasted only a few days in my dress pocket.

One day I realized I wasn't having nightmares anymore. And the only time I thought about Berlin and Hausberge now was during thunderstorms, especially at night. But Memme was always right there to hold my hand. She said she didn't like thunderstorms either and sat beside me with her mending.

People were happiest on Thursdays, when we got rations. Right from morning onwards, people smiled and kept looking out of the window. Everybody got rye bread, half a loaf per person. Only children under six years old got white bread. Ah, well! And because we were in the English Zone, the bread wasn't as white as some had expected. Listening to the women talking, mainly Mrs Peterson and Mrs Ott, I learned that they all wished they had been caught up in the American Zone instead, where there were 'prospects'. There were also a French and a Russian Zone, and it depended on where you were when the war had ended as to which zone you were in.

The rations, furthermore, consisted of a little cooking oil, some sugar, a little flour, a slice of sausage, dry peas, several tins of sardines, Camel cigarettes, and coffee beans. The last two items were used for money. Being the only child in the house, I alone got a box of sweets and a big tin of powdered milk. And sometimes the items varied to include condensed milk and other stuff, but I wasn't as much interested in the food as in the truck. It was a big army-type truck with the British tricolour on the hood, and I used to go to meet it, along with the First House Gang. As soon as it rounded the corner of House Number One, I jumped on the tailgate and hung there until it reached our yard.

Memme said hanging on to the back of the food truck was dangerous. The superintendent said the next time he caught me at it he would beat me 'to within an inch of my life'.

But I had made my decision. It was the only way I could challenge the Gang. And that's when I decided that boys were straightforward and that girls were devious.

Rein tried to push me away. But Erika pretended to run along with me, and then tried to trip me just as I was about to jump.

But while we hung on, we hung on together, and at least for that brief ride, I was a part of that Gang. It made me feel proud because sometimes Vello missed his hold or grabbed for air and fell. Or Tõnu's clog came off and he had to go back for it. Redhead Pügi hardly ever made it. When he did, he sometimes fell off into the road crying.

If Erika hadn't been Rein's sister, I would have tripped her too, once and for all!

10 Manure and Coffee and Silver Slippers

It was one of those butter-yellow summer days, with green-and-blue shadows and a cool breeze in the most unexpected places.

'Cat,' I said. 'Wouldn't you just love to do something!' But I couldn't think what.

Cat said she had some cat business to attend to. She didn't wait for me but streaked off by herself. She was behaving strangely, which Memme said was due to the full moon. 'Traitor!' I called after her.

Muki wanted me to stay and pet her, but Unki was resting his head again and Memme said it would be better if I went outside to play. It was a shame about Muki not being allowed out.

So I played hopscotch in the yard, in front of the main door. Hopscotch was a good game.

It was a very hot day. The doors and windows were all open. People were in the garden sunbathing or talking under the trees. 'Buzz-buzz-buzz,' they were saying, and I was dying to know what. Heads were together one minute and thrown back the next. 'And then she said ...' 'And then I said ...' 'You don't say!' it continued.

The Mölders and Petersons had brought out their chairs and tables and set them on the grass. They were calling each other from the kitchen or as they went by with covered dishes, with smells like sauce and onions or apple stew. It made my mouth water, just smelling them. We had sauce and onions all the time, but other people's food always smells better than your own.

I had no one to play with, so I played for two. Me, then 'her'. 'She' was losing, of course.

I was jumping for 'her', my back towards the drive, when I felt something cold trickling down my back. I whirled around in surprise, hoping it was Mrs Mölder spilling some red-currant juice or a spatter of home-brewed ale. But it wasn't, and I should have known better. It was liquid manure, the stuff they spread on the fields in early spring and summer. As I turned I got the full force of the jet right between the eyes. My scream was followed by shrieks of laughter, as three heads appeared above the German hedge. One boy was still brandishing the dripping hose.

Those mean German boys! I knew they had an open septic tank for their greenhouse. We could smell it. I wiped my face clean, thinking, 'drats' and 'rats' and worse things, but I didn't really get angry until I saw my dress – my new blue dress. It was brown and stinking all over!

That did it!

I grabbed the hopscotch stone and flung it right into the boys' stupid faces. They ducked. I heard a terrible shattering of glass. A greenhouse.

They turned on their hose again. I fought back with every stone I could find. In no time the yard was full of manure. As for the greenhouses, all I could hear was the breaking of glass. It sounded like music!

Suddenly I was hoisted off the ground, carried, and set down in the darkened hall. 'What do you think you are doing?' someone asked.

I looked around into a strange gathering of brown-streaked faces. People were running back and forth, clutching soiled blankets and pillows and chairs. The superintendent held on to my ear, and I knew I was in trouble. The summer buzzing voices had turned hoarse and angry, short and sharp. I got the tone, though the words came in snatches:

'Diplomacy ...'

'... already explosive situation with the Germans ...'

My ear was hurting.

'The need for caution and tact ...'

I had lost my best hopscotch stone. It would take a long search to find another as good.

'Provocation ...' thundered the superintendent. 'International agreement and regulations laid down by the committee ...'

It was building up to a spanking. I wondered when they would get around to it and who would do it, Mother being away. Three to one I wouldn't get it.

'But they started it,' said Memme indignantly.

There was hope.

'That's no excuse! She should have come straight to me or run inside. Any trouble with the Germans should be reported to the camp commander through the proper channels.'

It went on and on, all about the ruined blankets and things, the broken greenhouses, until the superintendent turned to Memme. 'You'll have to keep a firmer hand on that child,' he said, dismissing us.

In our room, I said, 'I'm sorry!' Not for throwing the stones but for Memme, for people having said it was her fault.

Unki came out of his room. He'd been cutting his corns and roasting onions to soften the skin. Putting roast onions on your corns, he said, made them soft. He took the onions out of the oven, from the ashes, but didn't say anything to me. Memme wasn't speaking either. She undressed me and started washing my hair.

'What a smell!' said Unki finally.

I could tell they weren't really angry at me, just thoughtful. While Memme scrubbed and soaped me, I kept looking at my blue dress, now a brown heap in a bucket of brown water.

When I was clean again and back in my green dress, Memme

bent under the bed and took something from one of her small bundles. She put it in her apron pocket and went out.

'Where's Memme going?' I asked Unki.

'To mend the greenhouses,' answered Unki. And he winked at me as in old times.

'Will coffee mend "diplomacy"?' I wondered.

'Coffee will mend anything right now,' said Unki, winking.

Sure enough, Memme came back smiling. She said all was forgiven and forgotten. I could walk by the farm again anytime and no one would hurt me. Then she started scrubbing the blue dress.

I went outside to look for Cat. She hadn't returned yet, so I climbed the pear tree to my secret nest and thought about it all. It was peculiar because *I* had been forgiven, although *they* had started it. *I* had been told off, Memme had been shamed in front of everybody, and my dress had been ruined. Yet, looking down through the branches into the window of the farmhouse, I could see the German farmer and his wife at their kitchen table, drinking our coffee.

I wondered about things like that often, and my heart would beat in my stomach. And I wondered whether my father was in Siberia.

And I wondered why it was that sometimes, on Sunday afternoons, I would come in from play and find Memme sitting and staring out of the window into the gathering dusk. When she saw me she dabbed her eyes and hid her hanky, but I knew that there was something going on that even grown-ups couldn't put right. Even coffee couldn't do it. And even Memme couldn't take care of it, the way she took care of everything else. That was the spell she had talked about – the spell that had been put over the whole world.

Cat was getting lazy. She saw me but couldn't be bothered climbing the tree anymore. She slept all day, and stayed out all night. What a cat! And she'd got her ear bitten. Unki said it was the full moon that did that. 'Just as it controls our own bodies.' And so I thought about that, too.

The best place in the house was the attic. There was no doubt about it. But it was so out of bounds that it controlled itself, because of the straw falling through the floorboards. As soon as I reached the raised platform, having taken every care in the world, someone would shout up, 'Who's in the attic?'

'Just a mouse,' I'd shout back.

So imagine how happy I was when Mrs Mölder got bedbugs. We'd all had them and suffered them, but she decided to take action. Unki had mixed some brew, which he said would 'hold back the Russian army'. He spread it on the walls, but it only made our room smell bad.

But Mrs Mölder complained 'officially', and we were told the exterminators were coming.

The superintendent knocked on our door and told us to move into the attic. We were actually to sleep in the attic one whole night and I could kick up a real straw storm if I wanted to.

I started straight up the ladder, but Memme got me by the back of my skirt and told me to wait. Things had to be packed first. Muki's cage had to be covered. Everything had to go, including the stuff in Unki's chamber.

I helped Memme until she said I was 'too much help', and she told me to run along and find Cat, so she wouldn't be left inside. Unki was already carrying things up the ladder, the stuff from under his bed, wrapped in his greatcoat. And Muki's cage, covered with Memme's petticoat.

'I'll see you later,' I told Muki, lifting the lacy hem. Muki, too, was excited and pressing the wire to get out. Her flanks were trembling and her nose twitched.

I found Cat sleeping on the toilet windowsill. I scooped her up and went into the yard to find a nice place to sit and watch from. I chose the Angoroffs' table.

The hall was full of people. Some were staying right there in the hall; others were going to sleep in the stables and the pigsty – rather than the garden. Most of the men were going to sleep in the garden, with buckets of beer and stuff. That was why the women said they preferred the pigsty. But everybody was in a good mood, hurrying back and forth, and taking things into the garden to be aired.

I thought I might go into the attic now, just for the fun of it, but then I thought, Why spoil it? Instead, I would pretend I still wasn't allowed. Then, when the superintendent came to inspect our room, to see if it was empty, I would say, 'Excuse me. I must look at our things,' and I would climb up the ladder right under his nose. And I'd take my time.

But Cat was still sleepy, curled up on my lap with barely an eye open. I couldn't take her with me.

'Your grandmother is calling you,' said Mrs Angoroff sharply. She was taking some blankets for hanging and spraying in the garden. She didn't like my sitting on their table, but where else could I sit and see what was going on? I had been told to go outside and play. Outside, I was told to go in. So I stayed put.

'Look, Cat, the exterminators are coming.' A van drew up in the yard. Two men in overalls got out and were met by the superintendent. Cat looked up and nodded.

I quickly covered her with my skirt, as the men came out of the house. There were five, including Unki. They gathered around the van.

The women stayed by the front door, talking and laughing. No one was looking at me or Cat, so I stood up to see better. They were taking things out of the van: big bags of powder, hoses, brushes and pails, and tiny little stoves. There was a lot of joking as the men removed their shirts and flexed their muscles. Each one of them was handed a brush, pail, and one of the tiny stoves.

The women made way as the men stepped into the house. Memme was the last one out. She carried a blanket and a small bundle. I realized it was too late for me to go upstairs.

'All out,' shouted the superintendent. The men in overalls had fitted cylinders to their backs with attached hoses.

The cylinders were taken inside and the front door was shut. We all moved into the garden. Memme spread our blanket under a plum tree. Everybody was talking at once. As suitcases and bundles were handy, it was a convenient way to show off one's treasures.

Mrs Angoroff started with her damask tablecloth. 'A wedding present from Russia,' she told us. 'The Czar had one just like it.' And she told us how the twelve napkins had been stolen, one by one.

Everybody listened intently, nodding and agreeing with every word impatiently. 'Yes, yes!' When she paused, she was quite breathless. Someone jumped in immediately, having waited for that moment. We were shown a mink stole. Memme said that mink is like rabbit, only more expensive. This one looked like a cat in mothballs. I couldn't see what all the fuss was about. The lady was keeping it 'for civilized company'.

Mrs Ott showed us her silver wedding slippers. They were so beautiful that I wanted to touch them, but Memme pursed her lips into a silent No. Ah, well! Mrs Peterson had a silk scarf 'from Paris', and showed us what was left of it. Just a bit, but it was real silk, she told us. Real silk was like gold or real money. It didn't have to shine or look good to be valuable. I knew these were real treasures then, even the mink stole, because people said so.

But as I looked at the faces around me, I wasn't so sure. When they said, 'Oh, how lovely!' the owner looked very proud but would then suddenly turn around and say, 'Oh, it's nothing! This old thing.' The mink was thrown back into the suitcase with disdain. 'I had another one at home twice as big,' the lady said. 'But you know how it was. In the panic of leaving, there was no time to choose.'

Then those who had said 'How lovely' would turn to each other secretly, pulling down the corners of their mouths. It's nothing really, they agreed, but their eyes were jealous.

I shook Memme's sleeve for an explanation. 'How could it be?' I started, but I barely got my mouth open. Memme pulled me up and said it was time to take a walk. She hurried me out of the garden and down the road. She wouldn't let me speak until we were on the way to the woods. Then I asked, 'Why?'

'Because,' she said shortly.

Cat caught up with us a few minutes later. She was refreshed and started chasing butterflies. Memme had placed Muki's cage near an open window in the attic. I wished we could have brought her with us. Cat would have looked after her, so she wouldn't have got lost. Memme said Muki would enjoy some fresh dandelion leaves for supper. There hadn't been any rain for ages, and the unpaved, rutted track was hard and dusty. It was dotted with dandelions, and crusted with cow dung.

The rye was so ripe it hung its head.

The road formed a tunnel through the rye, buzzing, sizzling, and airless. Memme walked slowly, complaining about her 'veins'. I ran either in front or behind, picking dandelion leaves or stripping ears of rye for Memme to mill between her palms. The grain kernels tasted like fresh bread, warm from the oven that was her hand, and a little salty.

We reached the wood. Memme found a tree stump in the shade, and we sat down to rest. Cat too. It was so cool suddenly. I could feel the perspiration evaporating. Memme opened the top buttons of her dress and wiped her brow. Cat was panting, her tongue was hanging out between her front teeth. She couldn't make up her mind whether to rest or to chase the birds that were chirping all around us.

I watched the sunbeams chasing through the trees and noticed that the leaves were turning yellow. The leaves were ripe too, like the rye and the grass. 'Like me,' said Memme, 'waiting for the reaper of all things.'

She opened her bundle and took out a book, some bread, an onion, and a green tomato. We ate in silence, listening to the birds.

When Memme said she had rested enough, she opened the book and started to read my favourite story. I sat between her knees. The story was called *The King of Mist Mountain*.

'Once upon a time there lived a beautiful girl named Tiiu. She was very lonely because she had no one to play with, and it was her job to attend to her father's horses. She spent most of her summer nights in the meadow, where the horses grazed on fresh cool grass, free of flies and insects, and as the early morning mist descended, they were the first to eat the clover still moist with dew.

'One foggy night, Tiiu met an old man, who turned out to be the King of Mist Mountain. He had a whole houseful of daughters for Tiiu to play with, and he gave Tiiu a magic brooch and told her that anytime she was lonely and needed someone to play with, she could blow on it and come to Mist Mountain, where she could play all day.'

The story was a long one, and I could see it all happening to me. In my imagination, I was Tiiu, of course, and the button on my dress was the magic brooch.

In the attic that night, lying in the straw, I was too excited to sleep. I could hear Muki nibbling in her cage only a few feet away. Cat's furry body rested against my thigh. Memme and Unki were snoring together, Memme wheezing and blowing, Unki rasping and tearing at his tonsils. I was afraid he was going to choke. It built up and up and up. But no, after a throat-tearing snort, he would start all over again from the beginning.

The moon was shining brightly through the attic window. Cat

stirred, stretched, yawned, and jumped on an old spinning wheel on the platform so she could see outside. She perked up her ears and was listening for that yowling sound that had kept us awake these past few nights. And then, I knew, she would streak out through the stable trapdoor or straight through the window to the pear tree to meet a big tiger-striped tomcat that was calling to her, and the two of them would fight all night.

Climbing from the attic the next morning, the first thing I noticed was an awful smell. 'We can open the door now,' said Unki. He started unsealing the masking tape. The smell got worse.

'You stay here,' he ordered. Memme and I stood back as he rushed the door with his shoulder. Holding his nose he crossed the room and threw the window open wide. 'You can come now,' he called, a little later.

I followed Memme over the threshold. The little stove was still smoking a bit, in the middle of the floor. And the whole room was covered with a shiny silver substance.

'Watch that you don't lick your fingers,' warned Unki. He handed us both a broom. Although the door and window were open it was hard to breathe.

Memme and I had to sweep up the dead bugs as Unki scraped them off the wall. Stripping most of the wallpaper. Their medicine-like smell mingled with the fumes as they rained down. They were all so transparent. Must have died hungry. I felt sorry for the baby ones, so tiny . . .

Suddenly Unki swore and stamped his foot. 'Why the . . .' Memme started up, shocked, 'Paul! The child!'

'The damn things are still alive,' shouted Unki, and he started stamping on the floor again.

I squatted down beside the broom and watched with interest as the corpses started to stir, revived by the fresh air. First one foot, then another and another foot. They were not sure they were all there. This was followed by a vigorous kicking and struggling. With a final heave, a bug got off its back, onto its feet and staggered towards the stripped wallpaper. There was still plenty left to hide behind and lots of cracks in the plaster.

Then we all started kicking and stamping. Memme lashed at the walls with her hat but it was no use. They were all crawling back into the walls to recover from the poison.

The house was in an uproar. Everybody was very angry. By nightfall the bugs were back and desperately hungry.

We sat on the table all night. With the light on. To avoid being eaten alive.

Actually I didn't care one way or another. If the exterminators hadn't come, I wouldn't have had my night in the attic. And they may come again, so that was something to look forward to.

11 The Dare

Memme says 'Winter will not remain in the sky!' So it was with school. It had to happen, just as fruit had to ripen and flowers grow to seed. I knew all about it, just as I knew I would never get to join the Gang, with summer nearly over. Two ladies had come to visit Memme. One was tall and wore a raincoat. The other was fat and short, in a crazy hat. The stork and the robin, I told Cat. Enemy agents disguised as birds again!

At least Cat was back to normal. I was afraid she would run off and get married, as a young lady named Külliki Heinkriis from Number Sixteen had done. She had gone off with one of the soldiers, maybe the redheaded crewcut who had brought us to the camp. It kept people whispering for days.

Right after the ladies' visit, school started. They had both been schoolteachers, and their names were Mrs Vallas and Mrs Kuimets.

Memme took me to school. She dragged me physically along the field path, reassuring me there was nothing to worry about. 'Every civilized person improves with learning,' she told me. But then she muttered on about how with 'some' even that doesn't help. She was referring to her in-laws again, whom I had never met, and she probably meant Grandpa's mother in particular. Apparently they had never got along.

School turned out to be just the opposite to what I had expected. It was neither good nor bad. It was indifferent. The classroom was filled with familiar faces. Monika was there. So was Erika, looking sullen and miserable in the blue cotton dress.

Anu was in another class. She had almost forgotten me and acted very distant.

I slipped into a back bench and found myself next to Vello and redhead Pügi. And to my surprise, there was Rein, who had been kept back a year.

But the best part of going to school was being able to go alone into the village at last. I could use the swing. I could wade in the reeds by the pond under the bridge. I was free at last!

Yet something was still missing, which would soon be put right.

As soon as the bell rang, I was usually the first one out the door. Sometimes the teacher came and stood beside me and pressed my shoulder down until the bell had stopped ringing. Then Erika got out first. And Rein and Vello and Tõnu, even redhead Pügi got out before me. And by the time the teacher had let go of my shoulder, I was already caught in the millstream of traffic and the Gang had disappeared. And even if the teacher didn't stop me, they ran away anyway because they knew I was following them. And they hid.

The cart track became my regular way to and from school, and I took my time. I picked dandelion leaves for Muki's supper, or lay down in the grass, absolutely still, so I could hear the ripe wheat ears rattle a little, as the field mice scurried between the stalks. Lying on my stomach or on my back, I felt a new calmness all over, but inside, as usual, it was like a bumblebee bouncing along the edge of the ditch, restless and thrilled. I wanted to join the Gang and had to find a way to do it. I knew most of their hideouts and where they went, though most of the places were out of bounds, like the canal. I knew they went to the canal a lot. And then I thought, Maybe that's where they are right now!

It was just one of those thoughts that go with a long afternoon, and I remembered that Memme had gone to Stadthagen to sell Camel cigarettes. Unki had gone to 'feed his mice'. And it wasn't that far, just a couple of miles beyond the German village, where the endless forests began. Luckily, one of my stockings was held up by a safety pin. The perfect fishing rod was just a willow wand away.

Fishing with Memme's bent safety pin, I saw the Gang up on the railway bridge that spanned the canal, as I had expected. But imagine my surprise, when they started waving. They were asking me to join them on the other side of the canal.

I didn't need a second invitation. I climbed up the bank in a flash, but stopped in dismay. It wasn't a real bridge, just tracks and girders with big spaces between the railway sleepers, through which you could see the water below. Far below.

I hesitated.

'You scared or something?' called Rein. The others started laughing and taunting me. Rein climbed up and stood in the middle of the track, legs wide apart. 'I know you daren't cross, so stop following us.'

'I'm not following you.'

'Yellow belly!' shouted Erika. If she weren't Rein's sister ... As for redhead Pügi ...

Yet if that little snot could cross those rails, it would be downright shameful if I couldn't!

'I'm coming,' I called. Jumping from sleeper to sleeper, I set out. I kept my eyes in front, but every few minutes, I would freeze, staring down at the deep water below. My heart was bumping with anger, fear, and tears. But as I got nearer the other side, I began to feel quite different. It wasn't so hard anyway, and Rein wasn't laughing. In fact, they all looked kind of funny, with their mouths open. Paralysed with admiration they were, I was sure of it.

I had barely reached the other side when Rein grabbed my arm, and we all tumbled down the bank together in a heap. A second or so later, a train thundered by. In my excitement I hadn't even heard it coming.

Rein's face was grey. 'I didn't know ...' he stammered.

‘You see, we crossed down there,’ said Tõnu, pointing to a footbridge farther down the canal.

I had been fooled.

Redhead Pügi started crying. ‘I know you’re going to tell my mother,’ he wailed.

‘You won’t tell on us, will you?’ asked Rein.

I looked at the frightened faces around me. Tell on them, I thought, so their parents could tell Memme I’d been down by the canal? They had to be kidding!

‘That depends,’ I said slowly, through clenched teeth. I wanted to go home to Memme. I felt sick. But on the other hand, here was my chance . . .

‘If you don’t tell on us, you can join the Gang,’ said Rein. Nods from all the others. ‘Will you tell now?’

I shook my head.

We hurried back to the camp together and then spread out, each entering separately, but not before Rein had told me how proud he was of me. He said I could start as corporal. There was no time for the official ceremony.

We had to go to bed.

12 Trouble in the Sauna

The sauna was in House Number Eight. I knew it well from the outside, but not so well from the inside. Memme had tried to take me twice, and both times I screamed so much she became embarrassed to try again. It was much less trouble to wash me in the basin, in front of the stove.

As it was, I had nothing against the sauna itself. It was great fun. Memme didn't know the real reason why I wouldn't go in and why I screamed so much, and it was best that she never found out. If she knew, she wouldn't go there anymore herself.

As a new member of the Gang, I went there all the time. We hid in a clump of gooseberry bushes up against the dressing-room wall. The dressing room was just a lean-to, built of loosely fitting boards, with big spaces between them for ventilation. We squatted in the bushes and watched people dressing and undressing. All the kids in the camp knew about it, and there was always somebody there. And sometimes the men came, too, on 'ladies' night' and chased us away, while they stayed.

When I saw Mrs Lepatree from Number Nine and her daughter Monika going up to our room, I smelled trouble. She was carrying a roll of towels and was visiting Memme. And I had the feeling I knew why. I was just climbing to my secret hideout when I heard Memme calling me through the window. I could have pretended I hadn't heard, that I was in the woods playing 'hunt the witch', but Mrs Lepatree was calling too. Mrs Lepatree was like a hammer with you as the nail, and you got the feeling she would not miss. And it seemed that her arms, with the sleeves rolled up, could reach right across the camp.

I went upstairs and found them waiting for me. 'I'm here,' I said quickly, before they needed to start looking around.

Mrs Lepatree was already rising. Then she sat down again on Memme's bed. Monika was beside her, hands in her lap, eyes down, pretending to be so good. She acted as if she knew what they were talking about. I had never forgiven Monika for letting me down so at Number Nine, when I had really needed her.

Mrs Lepatree expected a polite curtsy. I bobbed and she grabbed my arm like a vice. 'Well, then, as I said, two are just as easy as one, and it'll save you a lot of trouble. Just soap them and douse them in cold water as soon as they get out of hand. I know how to handle kids. You are too soft. Kids are like animals and have to be housebroken to become people. My Monika would be the same if I didn't keep a constant fist under her chin.'

Monika didn't even look up.

Memme went in search of a clean towel and a bar of soap. 'Be sure to bring them back,' she warned me. 'And don't go outside until you've cooled off. And don't drink any cold water.'

Mrs Lepatree said she would see to it all.

Memme dressed me in two of her cardigans. All the while she was dressing me I tried to signal to her that I didn't want to go. I shook her sleeve and tugged at her skirt, but she didn't seem to hear. 'And see you behave yourself and thank Mrs Lepatree for going to this much trouble.'

'But, Memme . . .' I tried in vain for the last time as she tied a shawl around my shoulders. I felt she was avoiding my eyes on purpose, even smiling a little. Mrs Lepatree propelled us to the door, Monika first. Monika did a quick curtsy and slipped out. I didn't have any other choice but to follow.

Monika was pretending she didn't know me. She was staying close to her mother. Mrs Lepatree walked so fast we had to run.

There was always a crowd outside the sauna, talking and

'cooling off'. It was ladies' night. I took a quick peek to the back of the building, and even that split second told me there was someone there. I was sure the gooseberry bushes were moving. The whole camp was watching, I was sure of it. If Rein and the others were there too, I'd die tomorrow.

I looked around desperately. The gate was open. I intended to make a break for it across the cabbage field, but Mrs Lepatree's hand was already fastened to my neck and guiding me towards the dressing-room door.

I'm not usually a coward, but I didn't want to do anything rash, because besides the roll of towels Mrs Lepatree had a bunch of birch twigs under her arm. Just one of those against your bare leg and you would be dancing!

The dressing room was full, but for me it was not full enough. It was impossible to see out, but I could feel how the back wall was blinking. Against the swish of underclothes and women talk, I was sure I heard a giggle in the planks. Choking sounds and silent laughter. Or could it have been the wind?

Mrs Lepatree alerted me with a sharp prod. 'What are you waiting for?' Monika was already naked and shivering beside her mother. Suddenly I realized why she was the way she was.

I undressed quickly, keeping behind people as much as I could, and then let myself be nudged into the sauna, the birch twigs tickling my behind.

Inside, there was nothing more to worry about, except getting dressed again. The heat always took my breath away at first. You stepped in and stood there gasping. After your lungs got hot you settled down and it wasn't so bad. Through the steam you could eventually pick out figures that became people, all pink and shiny with sweat or red and blotchy from birching. Mrs Lepatree turned a dark red right away and placed us by the wall, while she went for water. The eyes got used to it, too, after a while, and once you could breathe and see, you started thinking. Like how to climb up the 'stage' to the top, where it was hottest.

Mrs Lepatree came back with a bucket of hot water. She threw it over us and started scrubbing. It hurt. Memme's hands were always so gentle.

When she thought we were clean enough, she handed us both a birch twig and told us to sit down on the lowest step of the stage while she washed herself.

After that scrubbing, I was glad to sit down. We sat quietly, not looking at each other or talking. At first it was enough to watch Monika's mother lathering and getting more water, lathering again and going for cold water, lathering again and birching, while the sweat ran with the soap. And still she wanted more steam. So she went back and forth in the fog, emptying and filling her bucket. It got boring after a while.

The birch was burning my hand, and I wanted to do some birching, at least flex the twig a bit to see how much it would give. Or perhaps I would make a bit of steam myself by throwing water on the hot stones. I gave the stick a little twitch, just for fun, on Monika's back. The flex was great!

Monika threw a quick look into the haze for her mother. She was by the stones again, bending over, sloshing water from her bucket. The steam was rising, and I felt a sudden sharp switch across my back. Monika was smiling – still looking down, though, the rat! I knew I had been right about her all along. Being good wasn't her nature.

So now it was my turn to look at Mrs Lepatree. All I saw was a bending birched behind at the cold-water tap. I slashed Monika across the thighs. We looked at each other for the first time. We knew the game and the anticipation.

As Mrs Lepatree doused herself, Monika's birch caught my arm. I struck back and hit her face. But she was right there on my back, and the battle began.

I had to climb higher to get out of Monika's reach, but she was just as quick. As we went higher, it got hotter and hotter. Near the top, where most of the women were sweating , it was wet and slippery, and the heat was so intense that I had to close my eyes. Still, I couldn't let up. The switching continued in a frenzy. I forgot about everything else, even Mrs Lepatree.

Suddenly there was a scream. I thought it was Monika, so I lunged again. There was an angry shout. I felt the whole stage creak and sway a bit. It wasn't anchored to the wall.

A hand struck my behind. That wasn't Monika, I thought, and remembered with sudden soberness as the whole room refocused on Mrs Lepatree. But it was too late. The slow creaking became a full groan, like a tree coming down. Arms were reaching and stretching, the steps were full of naked women sliding and slithering as the stage began to slip sideways. Amid loud screams and shouts, it collapsed.

I fell softly into a pile of soft bodies. But I didn't stay there long. Strong arms yanked me out to the cold tap. The cold water cut through my skin, but that wasn't half as painful as the switching that followed. Monika's screams deafened my ears, till I realized they were mine as well. We were pulled this way and that way. Mouths were opening and closing all around, though the words were lost in the general din.

Finally we were pushed out of the sauna into the dressing room. Monika crawled under the bench while Mrs Lepatree dressed me, roughly, pulling and hurting. 'Wait till I tell your grandmother,' she hissed. 'Just thank your lucky stars you're not mine! It would be the strap for you, young lady!'

At the word 'strap', Monika started whimpering.

'The stage wasn't built properly,' I tried to explain. 'Even Unki said so. He said it was bound to come down eventually.'

A thump on the back was my only answer, before I was shoved outside, towards home.

Sitting in my secret nest in the pear tree, much later, I wondered about grown-ups. I knew I had been naughty. Everybody was angry at me. Memme. Unki. But this puzzled me:

In front of me, everybody was stern and frowning, but I'd

heard Unki and Linda's father laughing and retelling the same story with tears coming out of their eyes and rolling down their faces. And Rein told me his father had heard it too and that all the men were slapping their thighs at the brewery. Rein said it was almost worth a promotion for me. He asked if I'd done it on purpose.

I felt like showing him the marks on my behind: Mrs Lepatree's five fingers, and a few others as well. On purpose indeed!

13 New Neighbours

I was sitting on the well cover, tickling Cat's tummy the way she liked me to, the way I had tickled the Angoroffs' pig's tummy before I became too busy. But I knew everybody likes to be scratched, and everybody grunts with pleasure in his own way. Unki liked me to scratch his back, around the wing bones – where the wings will grow when we go to heaven. He always responds with things like 'Just a little lower' and 'Yes, that's perfect. Right there!' and 'No, a bit more to the left.'

A convoy of army trucks was cruising down the main highway from Stadthagen, towards the camp. Three of them turned down our fork. The rest continued straight on.

Clutching Cat, I ran to the fence to watch them coming. I knew something exciting was going to happen. Cat did, too. She was no longer purring but had pricked up her ears and her tail was twitching.

'Maybe extra rations,' I told Cat. 'White bread and sausage, sweets and sugar, or something even better called cornflakes.'

Mrs Peterson and Mrs Angoroff had come out of the house and were standing behind me, probably hoping the same.

I wanted to sneak Muki downstairs so she could watch. I had a new secret nest in the bushes, and it was so secret that you couldn't even tell it was there. Muki could come down in her cage and sit there, as if she were in a forest.

The trucks came to a full stop between our house and Number Sixteen. It wasn't rations at all. The drivers jumped down, opened the back flaps, and started unloading people. They were helped down one by one. Piles of baggage and boxes followed, and filled the ditch.

The new arrivals milled around each other, fussing and counting their belongings. Men, women and, I counted, five children.

This was just the sort of diversion I had been waiting for. Every day has to have a bit of excitement in it to make you remember it.

As we stared at the newcomers, they glanced at us. I remembered well how we had first arrived. It was good to feel I belonged this time – I was on the safe side of the watchers in my own front yard.

A hand touched my shoulder. It was Unki, standing behind me, picking his teeth with a safety pin. He had touched me to let me know he was near.

Among all the people and baggage, I had noticed a pile of bundles that looked almost like our own. I reached for Unki's hand. It was the biggest pile of bundles I had ever seen, beside ours. And sitting on top was a girl my age, just like me. And if that wasn't good enough, busying herself with the knots and ties was a Memme-type grandmother, except that she wore a scarf.

As I watched them, it was like looking into a mirror of the past. Right then I knew I wanted that girl to be my best friend, as I had never had a best friend before. They *had* to move into our house, into the empty room on our landing.

'Unki, Unki!' I shook his hand, but he was looking elsewhere. He squeezed my fingers in reply but wasn't listening.

The girl's mother appeared. I knew it was the mother. She was a strong no-nonsense type. She shouted something in another language that sounded like Russian, of all things. The girl jumped off the bundles in a flash and started helping her grandmother. I had a strange feeling that she had seen me.

I had registered with her. With my cat.

Suddenly Unki dropped my hand altogether. 'Hey ... Juhan!' he shouted, and jumped across the ditch.

A man – he was the girl's father – stopped what he was doing and looked around in surprise. He saw Unki and dropped his task. 'Why, you old devil,' he called out. The two men fell into each other's arms and embraced in the middle of the road. They got to slapping and punching and laughing and making greetings like 'You old goat!' and 'I'll eat my boots!' till the tears ran down their cheeks.

Finally they sobered up, and Unki sort of cocked his head to one side and I heard him whisper, 'Don't tell me you're married.'

Juhan put a quick finger to his lips and shrugged. They both winked, and Juhan put an arm around Unki's shoulder. 'Come and meet the family,' he said aloud.

This was the moment for me. Quick as a wink, I was next to Unki, holding tightly to his hand. Me too, I told him through my fingers . . .

Uncle Juhan tweaked my nose when Unki told him my name. First he said it was Rin-Tin-Tin, then Lotukata. Katrin would have been enough, but what could I do? The lady smiled and I curtsied nicely. The grandmother smiled too and the moment had come. I stood in front of the girl at last. She was a bit taller than me, and her hair was much longer. It came right down to her waist. I waited for her to speak, but she didn't.

'This is Cat,' I told her, but Cat broke loose and ran away. Still she didn't speak. She backed up next to her grandmother, and her eyes were yellow, just like Cat's. I thought she was very beautiful because I wanted to like her. There was so much I had to tell her too: not to be frightened of me, that I wouldn't hurt her, that this camp was peacetime.

'You can call me Lotukata too, if you want to. I don't mind.'

Still she stared back.

'And this is Leena,' said the mother finally. 'She doesn't speak Estonian.'

Leena's limp hand barely brushed my fingers, and her

grandmother's arms closed about her from behind. I understood that gesture so well. But didn't she know I wanted to be friends?

Uncle Juhan started explaining to Unki that Leena and her mother and grandmother were Russian, and how he had married her mother to bring them out.

All the same, I couldn't squash the disappointment. How could I make friends with someone who couldn't even speak my language?

Unki and Juhan sat down on the grass with a bottle. I didn't know what to do. '*Katze*' said the grandmother, pointing to Cat, now back on the well cover washing herself. *Katze* is German for Cat.

I nodded. The grandmother smiled, and Leena smiled a bit too. '*Meine Katze*,' I told them proudly. Leena had understood. She spoke German. We could speak German together.

Just then the superintendent and some UNRRA men called for attention. They started reading names off a long list. As each name was called, the owners climbed back into the truck. The first full truck was to take them to Number Eighteen.

All on edge, I had to find out about Leena. There were other children running about, but I had no interest in them. All the same, I couldn't help noticing a boy with big brown eyes sitting on a fancy suitcase. He was about six years or seven years old, and he was watching a girl of about five parading up and down in front of the crowd of onlookers. This girl had a stick under her arm army fashion and was shouting 'One, two, three. Hup, two, three', as she paraded past the line. Her voice was so rough and gravelly it sounded like a man's. 'Hup, two, three!' Mrs Ott got a neat tap on her big toe. I would never have dared to do that!

Before Mrs Ott could protest, however, a man broke through the knot of new arrivals and scooped the girl up from behind. 'Inge, stop that,' he yelled, and cuffed her so hard she fell down.

But Inge didn't even flinch. Her father smacked her some more, but as soon as he was done, she got off her knees, spat the dust from her mouth, and I heard her use a word that even Unki wouldn't use in my hearing.

On her feet again, she looked around aggressively for something else to do. She saw Cat by the well and without hesitation rushed over and grabbed her by the back legs.

'You stop messing with my cat,' I shouted. But Cat didn't like it anyway. With a hiss, she streaked up the pear tree, Inge right on after her. What a girl! My anger turned to reluctant admiration. She would have made a marvellous friend if she had been older.

The names were still being read. Leena and her family were assigned to Number Sixteen. Inge and that brown-eyed boy were moving into our house, Inge into that empty room on our landing.

What a letdown!

I went to sit by Leena's father and Unki. They were still sharing their reunion bottle, which was nearly empty, and talking about old times. About how they had been in the Foreign Legion together. About Africa and black people. About a place called Saigon, where Uncle Juhan said he had 'run his heels into the ground'.

When it was Unki's turn he started talking about his coffee mountains, how in Brazil there were mountains of coffee and gold. He too intended to get his share, he said. As I listened to them, I could see Unki in his army greatcoat, with his knapsack on his shoulder, climbing, climbing up those mountains of coffee and vanishing over the top.

The house wasn't mine anymore. It was Inge's. She was on my landing and in all my secret hiding places. She even found my route through the attic and all my nests. And she could use them anytime she wanted to, while I had to be in school.

On the way to school every morning, I passed through

Number Sixteen to see if Leena was coming too. I wanted so much to be her friend and couldn't understand why she didn't come. When school was over I went back, but still she wouldn't leave her room, just as I had been afraid to come out at Number Nine, I remembered. She probably was also afraid of being different. Sometimes I saw her curtains moving. I knew she knew I was waiting, and I wanted to tell her it was all right. Her grandmother came out sometimes and shook her head. 'She no come,' she told me. As I couldn't speak Russian, there was no way to explain. The grandmother knew only a few words of German.

And Inge was getting me down. She was like the plague, following me all the time, pretending I was the enemy, and spying on me. She'd jump out from behind corners and go rat-tat-tat, pretending to shoot me. I knew it was her way of saying she wanted to play with me. But I couldn't play with a five-year-old.

One day I wanted to think, so I went to my secret nest in the bushes. She was already there, lying back and watching the sky. I said, 'That's my nest.'

She said, 'So what?'

'Leave my things alone,' I said. 'I was here first.'

'Not today, you were not.' She laughed. 'Firsties is keepers,' she said, knowing full well I had to be in school in the morning.

Another time she jumped at me from the attic. 'Boo!' she said, then fled into her room and slammed the door.

I hated her!

The boy with the brown eyes wasn't allowed out of his room. He was a strange boy, so quiet and serious. His name was Väino, and he lived with his mother in a room next to the kitchen. Sometimes when his mother went out to the toilet she left the room door open a bit, and I could see Väino sitting on the floor by the bed, playing with an old cardboard box. It was always the same box. I wondered what he was doing. When his mother returned and saw me peeping she slammed the door shut with her foot, after giving me that 'shoo and git' clap of the hands. It sent me running.

The mother was a lovely-looking lady, though, like my doll Marie. Her hair was yellow – not like Leena's yellow, though – more like straw. And she didn't wear regular clothes, only a long silk coat. I asked Memme why she always wore that coat, but Memme said to mind my own business.

14 The Red Hair Ribbon

It was another one of those school days again and getting colder. Autumn was coming, and Memme said she wouldn't know what to do if we didn't have our own stove.

The logs were sizzling, the pine resin was popping. Smoke filled the room again, and the porridge was burned. Memme was shaking the clock and saying it had stopped. I was going to be late.

Suddenly there was a loud knock on the door.

Who could that be so early? Memme gasped and panicked. She reached for a hundred things at once and shoved them under the bed. 'Just a minute,' she called out. She flung a coat over her nightdress, smoothed her hair, and went to open the door a crack. It was Leena and her grandmother.

Memme let them in. Leena came reluctantly, fighting her grandmother's grip on her wrist. She was all dressed up and ready for school, her hair tightly braided and her face shiny from soap. Babushka, her grandmother, flopped down on Memme's bed exhausted, wiped her brow, and burst into a flood of Russian. I didn't know what they were saying, but Leena didn't like it and kept shouting 'Nyet, Nyet!' Even I knew that meant No. She was stamping her feet and carrying on. 'Nyet, Babushka!' she screamed. *Babushka* was Russian for grandmother.

Babushka flung her arms about in despair. Memme nodded in sympathy. I remembered my own first school day here and how Memme had had to drag me across the fields.

Memme turned to me finally and asked if I was ready yet. I pushed my plate of gruel aside and said I was.

'You're taking Leena to school with you this morning,' said Memme. 'Leena speaks German, so you should get along very well. And take her to Mrs Kuimets.'

I said, 'Will do.' Secretly I was very excited. This was what I had been waiting for all along, to become friends with Leena. I grabbed my schoolbag and was ready. What a bit of luck, too, being able to leave without finishing the gruel and having an excuse for being late!

'*Da. Da.* The German she speaks good,' said Babushka to me.

But Leena wasn't coming. I didn't know what to do. I couldn't force her. Leena started to cry.

Patting and hugging didn't help, nor did soothing words and caresses. But then Memme had an idea. She went to one of our bundles, rummaged about, and brought out a little package, which she pressed into Leena's palm.

It was a beautiful red hair ribbon, the most beautiful hair ribbon I had ever seen. Leena's tears dried immediately. She ran the silk through her fingers. Memme got her scissors and cut the ribbon in half, one for each braid.

The ribbon was something Mother must have sent from England. Maybe to be put with my Christmas presents. Surely it was meant as a surprise for me. How could she?

Memme tied the bows, fluffed them to perfection, and said 'There, now, doesn't that make you feel better?'

Of course it did.

'Aren't they lovely?' asked Memme of me.

I couldn't trust myself to answer. Nodding dumbly, I felt tears welling up in my eyes.

Memme put an arm around my shoulder and whispered, 'Don't shame yourself! Be happy to make someone else happy! You have dozens of hair ribbons.'

But none like that! Still I tried to smile and bear Leena's

sudden turn of pride. Already she was fancying herself and throwing me gloating glances from the corners of her eyes. She knew exactly how I felt. She curtsied and thanked Memme in Russian. Babushka was glad too. She talked even more loudly and said she would stay for a glass of tea.

Leena was ready now.

We set out silently. Not a word was spoken between us. I kept thinking of starting in German, but every time I opened my mouth I saw those hair ribbons bobbing up and down in front of me. Then I felt like saying something that would not have been nice.

As soon as we reached the school, I made up my mind. I was going to forget all about Leena once and for all. I would take her to Mrs Kuimets, and that was that. I would never speak to her again, not in any language!

We entered the gate, and I saw we weren't so late after all. Everybody was still in the yard, and we were spotted immediately – because of those hair ribbons, not because she was a new girl.

The girls inspected her schoolbag and her clothes. She had the UNRRA winter school dress on, a grey woollen one with long sleeves, which replaced the blue summer uniform. I wore the same one too. At home Memme was busy sewing me a trouser suit from Unki's grey army blanket and trying to get me a hat to keep my ears warm.

The boys didn't pay any attention to Leena at first.

'What's your name?' someone asked. 'I like your schoolbag.'

I wanted to answer for her or translate, but then an awful nastiness came creeping up on me. It said, 'Don't answer.'

As Leena didn't say anything, there was a pause, then an overall silence. 'Well, what is your name, or don't you have one?' a voice called from the back.

'They want to know what your name is.' I translated into German. Slowly and clearly.

Now the boys had stopped playing too, and silence was over

the whole yard. I looked at Leena's face and at the bright hair ribbons, no longer so bright. Her eyes were pleading with me to help her.

'Leena,' she said shortly.

'Latvian?' asked a Latvian girl.

'Lithuanian?'

'She's German,' someone whispered, and everybody drew back a bit.

'German girl!' a voice jeered. It was Rein. The cry was taken up immediately. 'German girl! German girl!' They all had their memories and started shouting at once.

'No, no, you're wrong. She's not German,' I tried to explain. 'Listen, she's not German. She's Russian.'

'Russian!' The shouting stopped abruptly.

'Russian!' As the word flew from mouth to mouth, there was an even worse silence. What had I done? I hadn't meant to. I hadn't! But there was no way to explain.

'Russian, dirty Russian!' the shout went through the bystanders, and there was no stopping them now. The whole school yard took up the cry. 'Russian! Dirty Russian!'

Mrs Kuimets came running from the schoolhouse to see what was going on. Leena was led inside weeping.

I was left with Rein, Tõnu, and the Gang. All my friends were waiting for me to explain what I was doing with a 'dirty Russian'. I could tell them I wasn't with her, that I had just been asked to bring her along, that was all – but I couldn't. I remembered my own arrival. I remembered how much I had wanted to be her friend. And then I remembered Hausberge and how, given the chance, I had been almost as bad as Lisa, if not quite as cruel as Mr Koch.

The Gang was waiting for an explanation.

I told them that Leena's grandmother and my grandmother were having tea together in our room. And I asked them, 'Does that make my grandmother Russian?'

15 Väino's Puppet Theatre

It seemed that I had got myself into trouble again, but this time it was more a 'lies have short legs, like deceit and deception' thing, and it had caught up with me.

So I decided to be 'good' for a change, and to play 'nicely'. I went around to Number Sixteen and knocked on Linda's door. 'Poor chest' was feeling a bit better, and when her mother heard we were going to play 'nicely' with dolls, she let Linda come over to our house. Leena came too and another girl called Hiie from Number Eighteen, who was Linda's friend.

We played with paper dolls. My mother had sent me a book of paper dolls from England, and the names of the dolls were Mary, Jane, Henry, and John. And their clothes were more beautiful than anything we had ever seen.

Because we were going to 'play nicely' and not make 'trouble', we were allowed to play in an empty pantry off the kitchen, and use it as a house. And suddenly, all the women were very nice to me.

The only person who didn't like my new mood was Inge. We asked her to come and be the daughter when we played house, but she stuck her tongue out. She sat on top of the stairs sulking and waited for me to stop this strange activity, because she wanted to join the Gang. And she wanted me to take her.

The toilet was right there too. I started noticing that Väino was constantly leaving his room. I was sure he didn't really have to. All I heard was a crumpling of paper and deep sighing. When he came out he stopped in the aisle between the pigsties and the pantry for a long look at us, standing first on one foot, then on the other, and weighing the thoughts in his mind, until his mother's voice summoned him back to the room. I understood he wanted to play with us, but Memme said he was not allowed to play with strange children. I wasn't strange!

One day he came right up to the entrance of the pantry and stood there. He wanted to tell me something in private. The other girls watched him suspiciously. The game stopped. Their mothers had warned them that as soon as 'rough boys' came around they had to run home at once. Väino was a boy, but he was so shy and quiet, they didn't know what to do!

Väino led me to the harness room and, making sure no one else was listening, he whispered his one great wish: to have a doll. Any old doll would do. His mother wouldn't let him have one.

I couldn't give him Marie, but there was that nameless victim of the bash on the head. I ran upstairs, past Inge, and got my paper dolls. Since we had only been using the clothes, I said 'You can play with these, if you're careful.' I followed him to their door and got another chance to peek inside the room. His mother was in bed with an uncle.

'Shush! Mother is sleeping,' said Väino. Unki had told me about the African sleeping sickness. He said it came from cows, and there were a lot of cows in the German farm next door. I was sorry his mother was ill.

I returned to the game, but my heart just wasn't in it. All this playing nice and becoming a better person got me a pat on the head from Mrs Peterson, but it wasn't fun. And every time Linda played mother, she was so bossy – 'Do this, do that' – like her own mother or Mrs Lepatree.

'I'm sick of this,' I said, and smashed my doll against the wall. It wasn't a doll anyway, but a potato stuck with clothes pegs. The other girls took theirs and went home. Leena would have stayed, but just looking at her made me feel ... ashamed!

I decided to play with Väino in his room. I felt sure I could slip in there without waking his mother.

Inge saw me first and was overjoyed. She rushed downstairs to meet me, wanted to know if the Gang was meeting.

I said, 'Later.' First I had things to do. I crept around the house under Väino's window and took a quick look inside. His mother and the uncle were still sleeping. Returning, I knocked softly on the door. Väino opened it without surprise and let me slip through.

The room was bitterly cold. It came as a shock after the warmth of ours.

They didn't have a stove. That explained everything! Now I understood why Väino's mother and her visitors entertained in bed. They were not sick, they were cold. Even Väino's lips were blue, and he was shivering.

'Let's play in the attic,' I suggested. 'It's cosy in the warm straw.'

Väino hesitated. First he had to get something. Groping under the bed, he produced that mysterious box I had seen him play with so often. 'Now we'll go,' he whispered, the box under his arm.

For a treat, I thought I would get Muki. Memme and Unki were out, and I couldn't see any harm in having Muki join the game from her cage, or in letting her romp around a bit in the straw, pretending to be a mouse. There were so many mice now in the attic, that it was hard to tell who or what spilled the straw into the entrance hall. There was always a handful in the hall first thing in the morning and no questions asked about it.

We climbed up through the stable trapdoor. It wasn't easy with the box, and Väino was no climber. Väino settled down in the straw while I fetched Muki. Then Väino opened his box.

It wasn't an ordinary box at all but a puppet theatre. It had everything – a curtain, scenery, actors. Väino busied himself backstage and set up the scene. The actors were paper dolls with thread tied to their hands and feet. 'I made it myself,' said Väino with pride, 'even the actors.' I could see now why he liked the paper dolls I had lent him.

It was very beautiful and I praised it too. Väino's usually pale face went pink and his brown eyes took on a sparkle. He put the actors in their places. The curtain was still closed. I had to sit in the 'stalls', he told me. With Muki.

So I moved a bit farther forward, the stalls being in the front. But then suddenly Väino came to the front and said, 'Ladies and Gentlemen. Today we'll do it differently.' He asked if he could tie strings to Mary, Jane, Henry, and John.

I wondered what Memme would say to that. The thought flashed through my mind, but I agreed anyway. I wanted the show to start. The audience was restless.

But Väino had still another idea. Suddenly he said, 'Let's burn the theatre down. We'll burn the old theatre together with the old actors, and then build a new one for the English Company of Mary, Jane, Henry, and John.' He said they would expect it, and before I could say Yes or No or We'd better not, he had a box of matches and the first prima donna was going up in flames.

I watched, fascinated. She burned as if taking a final bow. First her legs, then her whole body bent forward and curled up. Muki smelled the smoke and started butting her cage. It frightened me too a bit. Playing with matches wasn't allowed, especially in the attic, amid the straw. A barn had burned up recently, near the schoolhouse. Three of Unki's drinking friends had died there in the straw, and later all that was left was a black charcoal frame and a sickly sweet smell.

'I have another idea,' I suggested. 'Let's burn it down outside behind the house.'

Väino said No. It was the first place his mother would look when she awoke and found him gone. And then I remembered I couldn't go because of Muki.

Väino let another actor go up in smoke.

Just then, there was a sound at the attic door. Memme put her head around and whispered urgently for me to get down. She was clutching a handful of straw, but she didn't see Väino.

I told Memme I had been in the attic with Muki. It wasn't exactly a lie. I took Muki back. She promised not to say anything.

Väino's mother was still sleeping when we re-entered the room. We sat on the floor again. Väino said he hadn't finished. All the actors had to go. I didn't like it at all. It made me think of my nightmares, but Väino was laughing.

As the smoke curled towards the ceiling, there came a mumbling from the bedclothes. The Uncle muttered 'smoke'. Väino's mother's shoulder appeared, bruised and fleshy above the sheets. 'What smoke?' she asked.

'I have to go and eat now,' I whispered quickly.

'But we haven't finished!'

'Another time,' I promised. Väino nodded and shoved the theatre back under the bed.

A year had passed and it was autumn again. Another beautiful summer had come and gone. School started normally, but there was something wrong in the way people talked – about not having enough food. People were sick a lot. The rations had been cut in half. There was no more sausage or sugar and even less bread than usual. And no more meat.

The three pigs got fatter and fatter, and the only talk in the house was about pork for Christmas. Smoked pork and ham and pork sausage. The pigs had already been divided and promised and quartered and halved. Memme was to get two trotters from the Mölders for letting them have her potato peelings.

And when they weren't talking about pigs they were talking about coughs and chest rubs and herb teas. Linda's mother was a regular visitor to our house because Memme knew a lot of herb recipes and spent a lot of time outdoors with her basket collecting herbs and pine resin. Her compresses were always out on 'loan'. And she also made me drink the teas that boiled on the stove and misted up the windows. They tasted awful.

Cat was fine, but Muki didn't look too well.

She didn't even like dry apples anymore or dried carrots. She sat in a corner of her cage shivering. But Unki said not to worry. He said Muki was just lonely for other rabbits. And he promised to take Muki around to Number Sixteen. Uncle Juhan knew someone who had a lot of rabbits and he was going to find Muki a husband. Muki was going to get married.

I tried not to worry anymore.

One day, when I got home from school, there was a delicious smell of cooking, and a pot of stew was on the stove. I knew it was something different. 'What's for dinner?' I asked as usual.

But Memme was busy by the stove. She ladled the stew into a plate and said to sit down and eat before it got cold.

'I'll have to feed Muki first,' I said. Muki was home again. But Memme said No.

So I ate. It tasted good. 'That's meat,' said Memme. 'Fresh meat.' I had only eaten fresh meat once before, in Hausberge. Unki had taken me to a railway canteen. When we got back home, Mother was furious. She said we had eaten rat meat.

Memme was watching me with a funny expression. 'Eat, eat,' she coaxed between spoonfuls. 'Without meat you'll be ill.'

Something was wrong. She wiped her eyes and blew her nose a lot.

'What is it, Memme?'

She went back to the stove. I finished my plateful of stew.

Now to feed Muki, I thought. If she was going to get married she would have to put on some meat. Unki always says 'the fatter the bride the softer the ride'.

I undid the latch of Unki's chamber, but Memme stayed my hand. She led me back to the table and took me on her knee.

'About meat,' she began, 'and animals that exist to be eaten. Like rabbits.' She explained how Muki had been unwell and wouldn't have lived anyway. And how the new bridegroom had bitten her in the leg and the wound would not heal.

I tore myself loose of Memme's arms. I rushed to Unki's chamber, undid the latch.

The cage was empty!

The next day, I wrote a letter to Mimma.

Dear Mother,

I like the gloves, which I am wearing in bed. Muki is dead. She went to a daddy rabbit to get some babeis but he bit her leg and Unki sais a rabbit with a bad leg cant have helthy babeis so we had rabbit stew becos we needed meat. A boy at School says you went to get some cigarettes with your money and got lost. How did you get to England?

Your own
Katrin

I signed it with a kiss.

New Year's Eve 1947 to Spring 1948

16 Joy and Sadness

New Year's Eve had arrived. I was sledding on the road for the first time since I was sick. Everything was thickly iced over. Inge was still sick. Several men were approaching from the brewery, Unki among them. They weaved a zigzag line along the slippery road. Unki broke away from his pals to say hello to me. He lifted me onto his shoulders and showed off my new boots 'from England'. At the same time he whispered into my ear not to tell Memme I had seen him. I crossed my heart and hoped to die, and asked him to take me with them, but he put me down. 'Another time,' he said, which meant No.

Still, I had my sled. There was just enough time for another run or two before dark, before I would have to go inside. I flung myself on the sled, flat on my stomach, and shot forward like an arrow over the ice, right into the path of an approaching truck. There was no way to avoid it. The driver's face was desperate. The truck was already out of control, swerving from side to side. Its wheels were slipping on the ice. I knew it was going to crash, but where? On which side of the road? The driver was shouting at me. 'Out of the way!'

And then came another voice, familiar: 'Drag your feet!' Unki had come back.

But I couldn't drag my feet. The ice was too hard. My boots just slid over it.

And then I had an idea. I threw myself off the sled and rolled over and over and over, towards the ditch. My woollen blanket suit gripped the ice like tongs. I was safe.

Or was I? There was an awful crash and breaking wood sounds. My new sled was in a thousand splinters! The whining of the motor seemed to be right above my head.

Then came another crash, much louder. I thought I must be dead, but I was not. Unki's breath was beery as he lifted me in his arms and shouted, 'She's all right!' Memme was coming. Windows had been thrown open. People were running to help from all sides. The truck wheels were pointing at the sky, still turning. With its undercarriage exposed, it looked like an unfortunate tortoise that couldn't turn over.

People were crowding around the truck. Mr Peterson and the superintendent were trying to help the driver out of his cab. He was all right, too, but swearing loudly. Blood was coming from a cut on his forehead.

Unki invited him to our room to have his wound seen to. Memme said, 'Yes, do come in,' and wouldn't let him do otherwise. So we all went to our room, Unki's pals as well, 'to help'.

The driver was given some of Unki's 'spirits' to put on his cut. I knew how that would hurt, and cringed. But instead of putting the 'spirits' on his forehead, he lifted the bottle and took a long swig, then wiped his mouth and said, 'Aaaahh!'

'For the inner wounds,' said Memme.

The bottle was passed around, again and again. After all, it was New Year's Eve!

Memme and I sat on the bed. The driver, an Estonian, was talking about the accident. He went over it a dozen times: how he had braked but the brakes hadn't held, how the wheels had skidded. And how he had seen me suddenly shoot onto the road without warning.

Unki's pals settled around our table. The driver asked Memme to drink too and wiped the bottle mouth politely. Memme hesitated, then took a small sip. 'To your health,' she said and made a face. She told them she only drank for 'medicinal purposes'.

But the next time around, she took a little more.

'To the new year!'

As the bottle was pressed upon her again and again, and as it wasn't polite to refuse, she became quite pink and merry. She even forgot to make a face.

Soon everybody was laughing and having a good time.

Memme remembered a story from her childhood, about a local man called Beer Keg Willie, from the village where she was born. Once he had tied a hog to the front of his bicycle – 'It was the first bicycle any of us had seen and the last in our village until years later, when such things became commonplace.' It ended up in the duck pond, hog, Willie, and all. She said some people had walked ten miles or more to see that bicycle. 'Now they fly planes!' she said, and sighed.

The men started playing cards.

'Let us thank God that no one was hurt.'

'Amen,' said Unki, already dealing.

Instead of the schoolhouse, we started the new term in House Number Ten. There wasn't enough fuel to heat the bigger building. But the pond would still be nearby, and my boots were still shiny.

Back in school, I got a shock. All the teachers were new except Mrs Kuimets and Mrs Vallas. Väino and Leena were there. Väino waved to me from the back bench.

Wait till Rein sees my new boots! I thought. After school, we would go and check to see if the pond was iced over. But where was Rein? Where was Erika and where was redhead Pügi? I looked around.

The classroom was half empty.

Tõnu, too, was missing. Were they all sick? I wondered.

Vello was there but he looked different by himself. He seemed depressed, and even his cap looked sad, hanging on a peg behind him. I sat next to him and asked him what had happened. 'Have they all got the mumps?'

'They've gone to the American Zone,' he said. 'They went

right after Christmas. My mother wanted to go too, but I had the mumps.' He took off his glasses and polished them for a long time. I guess he felt it was his fault. His eyes were an icy grey and melting in the corners.

After school was over, I didn't know what to do. I had looked forward to school and to meeting the Gang again. I had made a hundred different plans in my mind. I remembered how I had first followed them and how we had enjoyed last spring in each other's company. I remembered how we had waited all year for snow and then for it to melt, so we could float oil drums down the swollen ditches. Now I wondered with whom I could sail. It had to be a boy; then if he fell in it wouldn't matter. If a girl fell in, she always ran home and told her mother someone had pushed her.

I'll go alone, I thought. Or I'll take Cat and Inge. We would sail to England and visit Mimma.

It seemed like a good idea. The only trouble was that Cat lately had been getting fat. Some sailor she would make with that big tummy! And I hadn't seen her for at least a week.

I moved off the school steps and started for home. I had decided to look for Cat. And I didn't have to look far. As soon as I opened the attic door, there she was – and much slimmer, I was glad to note.

'Well, you old so-and-so,' I said, and tried to stroke her. But she seemed different. As soon as I put my arm out across the ladder, I knew why. She wasn't alone. There were five tiger-striped kittens bumping around her legs.

Cat looked very proud. She came forward and bucked my chin. 'Aren't they lovely,' she was saying, purring loudly.

I stormed into our room and called Memme to come hurry and look. But Memme didn't seem too pleased. 'Yes, the kittens are lovely, but . . .' In fact, she looked quite worried. 'You know what will happen if the superintendent finds them. He'll drown them.'

Memme closed the attic door extra carefully and wedged it with a piece of cardboard to be sure. That evening I pushed a bowl of milk through and closed the door again just as carefully. Memme said we were waiting for the eyes to open.

So we waited, but not just for that. We were also waiting for the superintendent to find them. I knew he would, eventually.

A week passed. And another. One day I got home from school just in time to witness the hunt.

Mr Mölder and the superintendent had everything 'under control', and a heaving sack was soon taken to the pigsty for 'removal' in the morning.

I screamed for Memme to help. But this time she was powerless. She stroked my cheek and said I must try to understand. I couldn't understand. The bag was to be taken some fifty miles from the camp and thrown into a river. That way, the men were saying, none of the cats could find their way back, as cats so often do.

'Cat,' I screamed out in anguish, as I was sent from the kitchen and told to go upstairs. 'I won't, I won't,' I shouted back. First Tondu. Then Muki. The Angoroffs' pig. And now Cat, although I had known it would happen. I had warned her not to love me, and I hadn't wanted to love her, either . . . but I did. I did!

Memme couldn't comfort me, not this time.

'It's just no good,' I told her.

That evening I decided to go and sleep in the pigsty. I took my pillow and set it down next to the moving sack, from which came a terrible mewing and pitiful sounds of distress. Sharp claws and tiny blunt ones tried desperately to tear the sacking.

Memme was upset too. She had gone to the superintendent to beg him to change his mind, but he had brushed her off.

I tried to talk to Cat, but she wouldn't listen. She thought I'd had a hand in it, just as Tondu had blamed me for his misfortune. To animals, people are all-powerful. They can open a door and let you in and feed you or they can keep the door closed or kick you or let you die.

When I tried to touch Cat, she scratched me painfully through the cloth, her way of telling me it was all over between us, just as it was all over for her.

I wept for her and for Tondu and for all my other friends. Memme couldn't stop me from doing that, neither could Unki, though they tried to explain.

'It can't be explained,' I shouted back. 'I'll stay here forever,' I screamed at them. 'I hate people!' Then I moved back again to stroke the sack.

All the shouting and screaming was keeping the house awake. Mrs Mölder felt that I should be allowed to keep Cat, at least, that everybody had known I had her but had turned a blind eye.

'So there'll be more kittens?' stormed her husband.

Mrs Angoroff suggested that the superintendent take them to the forest and let them fend for themselves, but he wouldn't listen. And neither would Mr Mölder. He said he knew cats. 'They'll be back.'

Everybody was arguing now. Memme said, 'Surely you don't have to drown them all.'

'Enough!' shouted the superintendent finally. He said he wanted to hear no more about it. 'For peace and quiet,' he would let me keep one. 'Just one, mind you. The others are going to the river, and that is that!'

Mr Mölder opened the sack carefully and pulled out the first handful of fur he laid his hands on. 'For you,' he said, and tossed the warm body into my lap. Then he tied the sack up again, tightly.

'Just make sure it doesn't dirty the house,' said the superintendent sternly. And everybody went back to their rooms.

I knew this was the end of it. I had thought of coming back down during the night and trying to cut the string with Unki's knife, but even I knew when to stay ahead. I thanked the superintendent and promised to look after the kitten.

Still, my heart ached for Cat and the other four, Cat most of all. We had been such good friends, but as with most of my friendships, this one, too, had ended in tears. 'Good-bye,' I whispered to the sack. 'I love you.'

I couldn't sleep the whole night, holding the kitten in my arms. I wondered how he could sleep so well, so peacefully, with his mother and brothers and sisters all waiting to die.

Memme said that animals don't fear death, that they don't fear anything that isn't actually happening. The kitten was now warm and safe and, to him, that was all that mattered. Memme told me to go to sleep too. 'You can't alter nature,' she said darkly. 'Or human nature.' And she started to undress.

Memme suggested we call the kitten Pafnucius, or Pafnuuts for short, after a famous monk. Pafnuuts was going to live in our room, as there was no need for him to stay hidden. He was going to become a part of our family. I tied a loose ribbon around his neck, and I forgot my vows, because right away I started to love him.

Time started going quickly again. From pussy willows to spring flowers, it leaped along towards sunshine, racing the swollen streams and flooded ditches. I found an old oil drum and invited Inge to be first mate, with me as the captain and Pafnuuts as cabin boy.

Inge was so happy to be playing with me that you'd have thought she were captain! And she made a perfect sailor. Even when we had to scuttle ship and get wet all over, she didn't complain. Pafnuuts didn't either. He clung to my shoulder or liked to ride inside my jacket, with his head peeping out. And I liked to carry him for warmth. When our hands got very cold, we warmed them on his fur, and for me, he was like a little inside stove that worked without fuel, just with a little bit of milk.

The snow was melting in patches. In some spots it was all gone, with new green shoots bursting out of the furrows, covering the fields with a grey-green fuzz, while in another place there would be an ice palace of transparent glittering lace, slowly dripping the last of winter off its back.

The birds were returning. Memme pointed them out to me and I wished they would stand still long enough for me to get a proper look. 'There!' she pointed. But already it had flown. 'That was a starling.'

In the woods, the snowdrops were fresh and plentiful. Inge and I gathered huge bunches of them and brought them home. Memme put them into a jam jar. One day, we will have a vase again, I thought. A real glass vase!

The pussy willows were soft and furry, just like Pafnuuts! The ground was squashy, but in my English boots I hardly noticed it. I was feeling for the moss around the roots and for the little knobs on the bare tree branches that meant a leaf was about to be born.

I loved summer. But I loved spring, too, when the wind was so strong that I could lean on it and let it carry me to school, and the air smelled so fresh it tingled in my nose like peppermint candy – or like 'toothpaste', which was something new that my mother had sent us from England.

We got word that UNRRA had a new shipment of clothes. The warehouses were in the centre of the Camp, in the Latvian section. Near the doctor's office, where I almost lost my foot.

A thick barbed wire fence was drawn around the compound but the gate was open. Already from a distance, you could see the huge mountains of clothing. With people milling about them frantically, searching for what they needed.

Memme tightened her hat pin, gripped my hand and pushed us through, chin first. 'You need shoes,' she said. 'And a winter coat.'

But the shoe mountain was the hardest to get near. Also the chance of finding two shoes that matched was impossible. They were not tied together. When two people found a shoe from the same pair, they wanted both, but neither would give up the one they had found. There were fights and shouting because it was cold and the need was desperate.

Memme grasped my collar and heaved me up the nearest pile of clothes. 'Let's try here first,' she said. I knew what to do. I dug into the mountain of sweat and mothballs, grabbed an armful to my chest and rolled down the other side. Once I was clear, I placed the pile at Memme's feet for sorting.

She sent me back for more.

So, it went on until I got quite carried away. Memme had to drag me out by the seat of my pants. 'Enough,' she said. 'Try this on.'

I hated the trying on!

The coat sleeves brushed the ground. The collar buttons fastened by my knees. My arms ached from holding them out straight and my knees got weak from standing on one place. Memme's mouth bristled with safety pins and she was muttering to herself.

'That's fine,' and 'taken in here and here and here and here,' and 'a bit off here'. When she had done and was satisfied, she put me to guard them. 'And don't move,' she warned me, 'while I get the shoes.'

I sat down on the pile of new clothes to watch the people around me. Especially the arguing and shouting and tearing. Two women pulled the same skirt until it ripped apart.

Suddenly I spotted Leena elbowing herself through the crowds. 'Leena,' I yelled. 'Over here!' She saw me too and came to show me the handbag she had found. It was an evening bag really, for evenings at the theatre. Mimma used to have one. This one had golden edges and a gold handle. Enough to make me purple with envy. I don't know what it was about Leena, but she got the best things! If I hadn't been sitting minding those mouldy old rags I might have found it first.

I told Leena I thought it was cheap and smelly. 'I mean smell the mould.' I opened it and showed her the mildewed lining. 'If I were you I'd throw it back.' I advised her.

'Really?' Leena looked inside and agreed.

'It's got the green fever,' I told her.

'It does?'

'Infectious! You can give it to me. I'll take it back for you. So you won't have the bother.' I offered generously.

Leena handed me the bag. She said she was going back for something else. I had the bag! Then suddenly, a strange woman stepped between us. 'You kids don't need that,' she said and grabbed it. No please or thank you! We were left staring after her.

'I'm off now,' said Leena.

'No you're not,' said Leena's mother. We hadn't seen her come. She gave Leena a clout on the ear. And another, 'for leaving our clothes unattended.' Leena was hustled away.

I was left alone again. The woman with the handbag was nowhere to be seen. Drats! I was thinking of trying the same trick on her, about the infection. Or maybe I would tell her it was cursed . . . but then Memme came back with two shoes.

Both shoes were blue but only one fitted me.

'What a day!' she said. And hurried us back just as it started raining.

I was trying to solve an unsolvable sum and wishing Memme were there to help me, when Mrs Kuimets appeared at the door of the classroom. She looked straight at me, then whispered to the teacher. Mrs Vallas nodded and then beckoned for me to stop working, to get up and go with Mrs Kuimets. A sinking feeling gripped my stomach. Someone must have seen me, Inge, and Väino smoking behind the mill and told! I hadn't been smoking. Inge was the one. I didn't have anything to do with it.

But Mrs Kuimets was smiling quite pleasantly. 'Your uncle is waiting outside,' she said.

Unki? Outside?

I dashed across the yard to a big army truck standing by the gate, full of men. Unki was among them. 'Here, Rin-Tin-Tin,' he called, and whistled.

'What are you doing in there?' I asked Unki in surprise. 'Where are you going?'

But right away, I already knew. He was wearing his army greatcoat. His knapsack was over his shoulder. He had my Christmas scarf around his neck.

The other men were all laughing or joking. As Unki lifted me up, one of them said, 'Look, he's taking his little bride with him!' And they all laughed some more.

'I'm going to Brazil,' said Unki seriously.

'Brazil!' Yes, of course. To his coffee mountains.

Unki held me close for a long time. 'Look after Memme,' he urged into my hair, 'and grow up to be a beautiful lady.'

'Ugh!'

But Unki hadn't any more time. He pressed something warm into my hand – his penknife! – and lowered me back onto the road. He kissed my hands tenderly, a finger at a time. I knew I would never see him again, like all the others.

'Unki ...' I tried to clamber back on the truck, but Unki shook his head. The motor had started.

'But, Unki!' There were still a million things to tell him and to ask him.

The truck started pulling away, slowly. Unki lifted his arm to wave good-bye, smiling sadly. But his gold teeth flashed the way they always did. He was standing among the other men keeping his balance, hand raised. The other men waved too, some with white handkerchiefs, but all I saw was Unki.

I started running. Perhaps they would stop one more time. But the truck picked up speed. I got left farther and farther behind. Then it reached a bend in the road and was gone.

But I kept on running.

Unki's chamber became mine, which was no consolation. Without Unki it was just a room. Even the smell of Unki had gone forever. Memme scrubbed and scrubbed around the empty bed frame. She had opened the window and removed everything but the strings of dried apples. All Unki's tins and bottles were gone too.

I sat on the steps and watched Memme working, scrubbing and scrubbing on her knees, the smell of strong soap and fresh air adding to the emptiness. It was the end. There was no one left, just me, Memme, and Pafnuuts.

'Why?'

'He has his own life to lead,' said Memme. 'In peacetime, everybody has to earn a living. Your mother is in England earning our living, so that we can go there too, eventually.'

'But why not now?'

'All in good time.'

'Why can't Unki live his "own life" with us?'

But Memme said she was busy, that 'everybody had to live his own life'. And she told me to start handing her the bundles. They were going into Unki's room. Pafnuuts needed feeding. I had homework to do.

I was just thinking about Cat and her misfortunes, when I thought I saw her across the road from our well. It wasn't possible! I called, 'Cat! Cat!' as I ran towards her.

It *was* Cat. She heard me, stopped for a moment and lifted her tail, then looked at me in terror and darted away. I couldn't follow her as she made for the German farm and slipped under their fence.

It just didn't make sense. Why? I went and asked Memme. But Memme told me to leave Cat alone. For her to come back like this was a miracle. The river was at least fifty miles away.

She must have suffered terribly, and she hadn't forgotten or forgiven. And now she was afraid of people, especially of people in our house. She must have come from the German farm in the first place, before deciding to live with us. 'It's better this way,' Memme concluded. She said I had my own cat now. 'Leave the mother alone.'

I couldn't believe that Cat still blamed me for what had happened. I had tried to explain. I had never hurt her. There was no reason for her not to trust me. So I had a plan. I would take Pafnuuts back to his mother and let him explain the situation to her in cat talk.

Pafnuuts was taking an afternoon nap, but I said it was urgent. I took him to the fence where Cat had gone under and started calling 'Cat!' Pafnuuts knew what to do.

I didn't have to call for long. Cat appeared suddenly a little farther away. But instead of rushing over to say hello to her son, she turned peculiar. Crouching low on her haunches, she stared at Pafnuuts as though he were a stranger. And an enemy.

Pafnuuts was afraid.

Mother and son glared at each other, and Cat's fur was rising. 'Shame on you! You're a bad pussy cat!' I told her. But she wasn't listening at all. She gathered herself lower on her stomach, ready to spring. And then, spitting and with claws flying, she attacked her own son.

It was all I could do to get Pafnuuts out of the way into my arms. Cat ran off, still hissing.

Inge came and asked what was happening.

Together we tried to puzzle it out. It was all very strange and unbelievable – like when I had heard Unki telling Memme that Muki's health problems had started with a broken leg. When I asked how that was, Unki had explained that the bridegroom had attacked her. 'Now imagine,' I told Inge, 'animals fighting together like human beings. And did you ever see a cat purring for another cat?'

Inge said she hadn't. 'They just purr for us.'

'Because we feed them.'

'Animals live in fear all the time of being eaten up,' said Inge. 'They can't relax.'

'The Angoroffs' pig was so relaxed when they cut him that he didn't even squeal. I saw it as I was running out of the house. He probably thought it was a broom scratching him when they stuck the knife between his ears. He just grunted and collapsed.' But then, of course, they had been in a hurry.

'Was there much blood?' asked Inge.

'It spurted out like a fountain.'

'I wish I had seen it,' said Inge.

'Memme told me that, in the cosmos, everything gets eaten up eventually. It doesn't matter.'

'Glass too?'

'I guess so.'

'My dad says Dog eats dog.'

'Hey, maybe we can get ourselves a dog,' I suggested.

With such a situation on our hands, we forgot to worry about anything else, such as where we were standing, or that we were out of bounds, on the wrong side of the road. The German boys had already seen us and were circling in from different directions.

Suddenly a rough hand gripped my collar and another my leg. With a chant and a heave-ho, I was lifted into the air and dumped into the middle of a large rain puddle. Inge came flying down on top of me.

The German boys pranced around, clapping their hands at our muddy faces and stamping at the edges of the puddle to make us even wetter. Inge's nose was bleeding badly. I couldn't get the mud out of my eyes.

Inge's eyes, however, were burning brightly through the muddy mask. I felt like crying, but not she. She was hopping mad. 'Filthy Fritzes,' she screamed back, shaking her fist.

Then I saw what they were going to do next. The biggest

of them had Pafnuuts by the tail and was swinging him around and around his head, faster and faster, and moving closer and closer to our house. As the others shouted encouragement, he raised one leg, took aim, and then let go. Pafnuuts flew through the air towards the brick wall until . . . splat! Like a ripe tomato, he burst open and was dead.

The boys started walking back to the farm, already laughing again and talking about something else.

Sick and stunned, Inge and I sat in our puddle. I watched them go, helplessly. But not Inge. Not for long.

'Murderers!' she screamed, and before I knew what she was about, she was out of the mud and after the biggest of them, the one that had killed Pafnuuts. I wanted to go too, but I wasn't as brave as Inge. I said she was special. So I stayed behind.

With a leap, she was on his back, her fingernails in his eyes. He wasn't even sure what hit him. By the time he had freed himself and Inge had landed back beside me, we were glad to see his face was bloody too. 'Got him right on the *Nase!*' said Inge, spitting out her own blood and lapsing into German. *Nase* is German for 'nose'.

'They're going to kill us now, I think!'

But instead, they seemed surprised and hesitant. There followed a short discussion, and then they left, probably because they heard Mr Mölder's voice, and that of Inge's father, who were running out to see what was going on.

In my room again, I could hear Inge's father shouting and the sound of his hand on bare flesh. Inge was getting a belting, for 'good measure'. But I was so proud of her and I knew everybody else was too, including her father. And I felt a little ashamed of myself. 'Why, she's barely six years old!' said Mrs Ott, who had seen it all from her window before calling the men.

I was sorry now I hadn't taken Inge to meet the Gang. She would have made a fine officer. The best. Maybe even a sergeant major.

Memme made me drink some valerian tea to calm me before we buried what was left of Pafnuuts. We buried him in my secret wood in a plywood box labelled 'Havana'.

When it was all over, I climbed up into my secret nest in the pear tree, but I wasn't hidden. The leaves hadn't grown yet. I felt exposed and cold. I had believed in the magic bubble between us and the rest of Germany, between us and the German farm, because I had also believed in the magic of coffee beans and a pound of sugar, a side of bacon and a pack of American cigarettes. Those things could mend greenhouses and stop quarrels, but they couldn't bring back a life. They were all gone now. There were just the two of us now – Memme and me.

I climbed down quickly. I ran into our room and hugged Memme and hugged her so tightly that she fell over on the bed. And then we sat at the window together. It started to rain.

One morning I went into the woods to look at Pafnuuts' grave, and I found it grown over with white flowers.

17 Good-Bye Again

It takes a lot of concentration to put an image down on paper the same as it appears in your head. I couldn't remember whether Cat had a black mark on her nose or just under her left eye.

Mrs Vallas said it didn't matter. 'A cat's a cat!'

But it did matter. As for Tondu, I couldn't even remember what he'd looked like anymore, except that he had been black.

While I was trying to remember a cat by face, I heard someone call my name. It was Mrs Kuimets, who was by the classroom door again! My heart stopped. Who was it this time?

There was only one left, Memme! I dashed for the door, but Mrs Vallas stopped me. 'Take your things with you.'

I stuffed my notebook and drawings, pencils and books into my schoolbag.

'The ink too.'

The ink too. And my hat.

'Quickly,' urged Mrs Kuimets from the door.

There was no time to look around.

'Run straight home as fast as you can.' She gave me a slight push. 'As fast as you can, hear!'

I didn't need urging. Fear and questions spurred me on. Was Memme sick? Had Mimma come back? Or Unki? Or, the greatest fear of all, had Memme gone to 'live her own life', too, and left me alone?

The field path had never been so long. I hardly noticed that it was raining, or that the new goose at Number Sixteen chased me across the yard.

A big truck was standing outside our front door, just like the ones Mimma and Unki had left in.

'Memme!' I screamed in desperate terror, and I jumped up to look inside. It was empty.

But the hall was full of people, in various states of excitement. 'Here she is,' someone called out as I appeared.

Memme took me by the hand and led me upstairs. She had her coat on and her hat. Something was really happening. 'Eat something quickly,' she ordered, pushing me to sit down at the table, 'while I finish packing.' All our bundles were out on the floor. There was our red knitted blanket bundle, the thick UNRRA quilt bundle, Memme's old coat bundle, my baby-blanket bundle, and about three new ones. I also saw a pail with brushes, two baskets of cutlery and dry food, cardboard boxes, and little tins marked 'Cardamom' and 'Chest Rub', and one marked 'Nestle's', whatever that meant.

'Where are we going?' I asked between mouthfuls.

But Memme hadn't time to tell me right away. Mrs Ott came in to say she would take something down for us, if it was ready. She told us the driver was waiting.

Memme said, 'Yes, yes,' her mouth full of thread. 'Thank you.'

Inge's mother came to the door too. She stood watching us, arms folded. 'What a rush!' she said. 'Just one hour, it's unreasonable.'

I asked if I could see Inge. 'Not now,' she said. 'Inge is taking a nap.'

'But I want to say good-bye.'

Inge's mother could see I was getting upset and agreed finally to let me in through the door, so I could whisper good-bye. But I mustn't wake her. 'It will be best that way, or she will be too upset.'

Inge upset? Then she must love me as much as I loved her. As much as I had loved ... all the others. And just as I realized this, it was time to say good-bye again!

Memme had to go downstairs. I followed Inge's mother to their room and stood by the bed. Just for a minute. Inge was fast asleep. I wanted to cry, so I took leave as quickly as I could. Silently.

Then I ran down the stairs after Memme. I knew I would never forget Inge and would love her as long as I lived.

Väino was in school. I hadn't had time to say good-bye to him. Nor to Leena.

From the talk, I understood that we were going to England to join Mimma, at last!

Mrs Angoroff was stationed by the stairs and kept saying 'How exciting' every time Memme went by, and 'Our son is in England. You must look him up.'

While the truck was being loaded, I ran back upstairs to our room for a last look. By that time I had realized we wouldn't be back, and for once, I wanted to leave properly. Even so, it was a shock to see the room empty. Everything was gone but the stove and the furniture and the soup kettle, which Memme had forgotten, or couldn't carry because it was hot. Well, here it was again, 'our room' but not our room anymore! I had come up to see if it was changed, and it was. At Unki's chamber door I said, 'Good-bye, Unki's chamber,' and pacing from there on, I systematically eliminated all that had been 'ours' again. 'Good-bye, attic door; good-bye, attic!

'Good-bye, stage and spinning wheel.

'Good-bye, ladder.'

Memme came back for the soup kettle and said, 'Come on.'

'Good-bye, landing!'

I dared not look at Inge's door. 'Good-bye, stairs!'

Memme called for me to hurry. 'What are you doing?'

'Good-bye, hall!'

Everybody was standing in the yard around the truck. The driver was sitting on the running board smoking a cigarette. The bundles were being thrown from Inge's father to Mr Mölder, who passed them to the superintendent, who packed them 'in'.

The women were shaking Memme's hand and wishing her a safe journey.

And there came Babushka running across the road, her skirts flying. She and Memme fell into each other's arms, with the soup kettle between them.

Babushka stroked my cheek and said good-bye to me in Russian. I was able to answer her and felt very proud. Then the two grandmothers kissed each other again, crying and laughing at the same time, until the driver threw away his cigarette. It was time for us to get in. He fastened the back of the truck.

While the people were pressing close for a last handshake, I noticed Mrs Ott holding our coffeepot. Mrs Peterson had a string of our apples around her neck and parts of our stove around her wrist; namely the cooking rings. And then I remembered my scooter. It was in the pigsty. If someone was to get it, it had to be Inge. I grabbed Memme's sleeve and whispered to her urgently. She called Inge's father to the side and said I wanted Inge to have my scooter. I felt she was the only one worthy of it.

Now that was settled, I was ready to leave. My biggest heartache was less bad now. I knew that when Inge woke up and found me gone, she would be upset, but that when she saw the scooter, it wouldn't hurt quite so badly.

The motor started up. Suddenly Memme realized she was still clutching the soup kettle. As the truck started moving, she thrust it against Babushka's chest. 'The soup is still warm,' she called, as we rounded the corner.

'Good-bye, house!

'Good-bye, mill!'

I wished I'd had a chance to do this when we left Estonia.

'Good-bye, secret pear tree!

'Good-bye, Number One House!' And silently, 'Good-bye, Gang!'

We were already turning towards Stadthagen. I had a last

glimpse of the church steeple, 'my' woods, and 'my' fields.

It had happened so quickly, but for once, I was keeping track. Just this morning, I had been sitting in the classroom, drawing Cat from memory, and suddenly the whole camp had become memory. I thought it was all tucked in my mind, safe forever: the smell of dried apples in Unki's chamber; the torn blue wallpaper of our – no longer our – room; the streaked white-washed walls of the pigsty, and the crumbly, fine mud of its hard-packed dirt floor; the raggedy straw sticking out of the coarse-woven mattresses, smelling of bed bugs; our door. What colour was our door? I had already forgotten.

'Memme, what colour was our door?'

'What door?' asked Memme. We were sitting on the bundles, trying to keep our balance as the truck twisted and turned, tossing us from side to side and bouncing us up and down on the same potholes that had brought us into the camp.

'An hour,' grumbled Memme. 'They gave me just one hour to pack! Half an hour, if possible, they said. I don't even know if I have everything.' And with that thought, she began to worry, fret, and recheck the bundles. Count the sheets and towels. The tablecloth was missing. No, it wasn't. There should be five forks, six knives. Her hat fell forward across her eyes, and since she wasn't really talking to me, I didn't have to answer.

Instead, I watched the passing scenery, what I could see of it between the back of the truck and the overhead canvas. Roofs, trees, open sky, and telegraph wires. Were we driving straight to England? I wondered.

Memme said my mother would be meeting us 'at the station', which had to mean a train station. In school we had learned that England was 'across the Channel', so somewhere we would have to board a boat as well. Actually, I had no idea where England was, and I wished now I had listened more carefully in class instead of picking bugs out of the hem of my dress. But wherever it was, I called out to the sky, 'Mimma, we're coming!'

My bottom was getting sore from the bumping.

Memme had finished checking her bundles and was sitting staring at the canvas walls, a stunned look on her face. She patted my knee when she heard me, knowing I hadn't understood Mother's having to leave in the first place. All the letters and parcels and promises had still kept us separated. The way I saw it, if you love someone, you want them near, so you can touch them and see them whenever you want to.

Memme returned to that vacant look. 'I shouldn't have given away the coffeepot,' she said at last. 'I'm going to need it. It had a good strong handle.'

I must have fallen asleep. When I woke up, it was with a jolt. The truck was standing still. Artificial lights and men's voices surrounded us. I crawled to the back flap to take a look and got a fright. There were soldiers out there with rifles.

Memme took my hand and said it was all right. They were guards.

She straightened her hat and buttoned her coat.

'We've arrived,' she said.

'In England?'

'No, at the transit camp.'

18 Another Camp!

Another camp! Not that I had anything against camps anymore. But I hoped we were going straight to England.

This camp was different, more what I had expected the first camp to be like. It was enclosed by barbed wire, and instead of houses, there were rows and rows of wooden barracks. Every barrack had a lamp over its front door, and the entire camp was brightly lighted by tall lampposts.

There was only one gate. Our truck had stopped at it. A red-and-white-striped pole barred the entrance next to the guard hut and sentry box. There were some other huts nearby. The electric lights were humming strangely. The same kind of humming was also coming from one of the huts.

Outside the wire fence it was pitch-black with a faint outline of trees. The ground was wet. There were rain puddles, and boot prints were sunk deep into the brown mud.

The driver had gone into the office with a sheaf of papers. Memme was called in a little later.

The sentries, or guards, were all speaking English, and I wished I could understand what they were saying. This must be what it is like to be in England, I marvelled – everybody speaking English! Again I wished I had paid more attention to that 'What is your name? My name is Mary' stuff. It really was a shame.

Left alone, I felt sleepy again, with a terrible urge to go to the toilet. But where? I couldn't see any toilets. The woods were too far, across the fence. With all those lights, the soldiers would see me if I squatted down beside the truck, and our potty was in one of the bundles – I didn't know which one.

There was no way. So I pressed my legs together and waited for Memme to come back. Rocking back and forth helped a bit too.

One of the soldiers looked over the flap and smiled. He said something that ended in the word *kid*. A few more faces appeared. 'Hello!' they said.

'Hello!' I replied, and decided that just as all American soldiers chewed gum, all English soldiers were thin and had big ears. It was one of those things!

As soon as they had gone, I decided to climb down. One of the barracks had a dark area close to the fence. It looked convenient.

Climbing over the back was agony. Each movement was like a knife deep down. I wondered why the guards had rifles. Was it to shoot with or just to drill? What would happen if they heard me out there in the darkness, didn't know who I was, and maybe mistook me for a Russian? It was a sobering thought. I stood in the shadow of the tail of the lorry, one foot pressed on top of the other. Going into the bushes had never been a problem, but the rifles kept catching my eye. It was dark out there and so light here. No in-between. If they shouted, 'Who's there?' I could say I was a rabbit. But puff, bang ... I might still be dead anyway.

'Hey ...!'

A sudden hot spring flooded my trouser leg. To my horror, like a baby! It was only Memme and the driver coming back. The driver called 'Hey!' again and waved.

I climbed back into the truck as fast as I could. One puddle looked just like another in that light. The blanket suit was like a blotter, but the wet leg was turning cold.

Memme didn't notice anything. She climbed back in and said, 'That didn't take long!' The driver patted me under the chin. I was probably looking miserable.

At a signal from the sentry, the barrier was raised and we

drove into the camp. Then we stopped again in front of one of the barracks.

Before anyone could lift me down, I was down and out of reach.

Two soldiers appeared and started unloading our bundles. We were shown into the room. The whole barracks was just one room. I got the impression of a railway carriage lined with bunks. People's heads lifted as soon as we entered and stayed propped, watching us. Our bundles and boxes were thrown into one corner, beside the stove and two empty bunk beds.

'Can I take the top one?' I asked Memme hopefully.

The straw mattresses had to be filled first, though. It was the same routine we had gone through before, and I knew just what to do. Memme took off her coat. I was just about to clamber up the ladder anyway, when I heard my name being called. My real name, not Lotukata or Rin-Tin-Tin. It gave me quite a start.

'Katrin. Over here!'

Having your real name called when you've got wet trousers is bad enough, but it was even worse when I saw who it was. Memme saw them too. Viive Kotipuu, none other, from Haapsalu, with her aunt, Miss Taras. Well, how about that!

While Memme and the aunt kissed and embraced, I had to think fast. Viive and I had never really got on that well. I had been glad to see the end of her. But here she was, climbing down from a top bunk to ply me with questions: Where and what? I climbed back down too and kept my distance. There and that, I answered. I asked if she had had to leave her toy post office behind. We had always quarrelled over that post office of hers, which had real money in the till, and over the pony, which she wouldn't let me ride.

Viive didn't want to talk about the pony. She warned me it would be lights out in five minutes. Her aunt told us to hurry. There wasn't time to fill the mattresses.

Memme spread our bundles evenly on the floor and said,

'We'll sleep right here.' She'd barely got my boots off when the lights went out.

Memme was sleeping in her overcoat. I was fully dressed too, but my soggy trousers were chafing me and felt uncomfortable. The more I moved, the more they rubbed, and I was getting terribly sore. Finally I rolled over to Memme and whispered my shame.

Memme wasn't angry. She only wanted to know why I hadn't told her before. She groped in the bundles for an extra blanket, made me take off the wet trousers, and hung them over the stovepipe. I was sure everybody could see. It was like sleeping in the middle of a road.

There was breathing all around us. Heads were down now, but the bed sacks were rustling constantly. Bed boards were creaking. People were scratching and coughing, sighing and snoring. There were low whisperings, nose blowing, searching for things, dropping things. Getting up, going out, and coming in. Someone stood on my foot and said, 'Sorry!' A baby started to cry.

One of the outside lamps was shining straight into my face like a full moon. There was something crawling along my arm and biting.

Morning came as a shock. I wondered where I was, as a pair of legs stepped over me and then another pair started to follow. I had rolled into the centre of the floor. Memme was up already. She handed me my trousers. I was grateful to her for having removed them from the stovepipe before anyone could see them.

When I pulled up my sleeve, I saw that my arm was full of bites.

'The bugs here are terrible,' said Viive's aunt.

Memme handed me my toothbrush, towel, and soap.

Viive was very snooty that morning. With reason. She knew her way around and I didn't. She had been here a whole month already.

By the time we reached the pump, she had told me exactly where and how to stand and how to work the pump so the water wouldn't come out too quickly. I dabbed my face, then rubbed it red with the towel. That way it looked washed. I had noticed a terrible stink around the pump and asked Viive what it was.

'Oh, those are the latrines,' she explained importantly, 'and the smell is lime. You have to hold your breath from when you go in to when you come out. Can you do that?'

I said I would try. I took a deep breath and dashed inside. It was awful! My chest started hurting and my eyes watering. I could hardly see where I was going. There was deep mud all around and a ditch behind the wooden bar. I knew you had to sit on the bar, but it was too high for me. I did my business as best as I could and bolted for the door and fresh air.

Viive greeted me with hoots of laughter.

'Those are the men's! The women's aren't that bad.'

Well, Viive Kotipuu, I said under my breath. Seeing it's going to be like that with us . . . to you too!

19 The Horror in the Woods

It was time for breakfast. Viive and I had to stand in the food line, which was so long that it reached halfway across the camp. Standing in that line with Memme's enamel bucket, I thought this was a fine camp, much more exciting than the last one, because we were all together. I liked it when people were all in the same room together. It was safe and warm, and there was always someone to look at.

The sun was shining brightly. The puddles between the barracks reflected the sky and were blue. The woods around the fence had a springtime fuzz of new leaves. There was dew on the still-naked branches and on the barbed-wire fence. A freshness in the wind drove away the musty straw smell and the lime and pee smell that hung over us.

I wondered what was beyond the woods, beyond the tall pines that formed a wall against the outside world. I thought I heard a train whistle, and planes flying low, landing somewhere close by. There were also railway tracks beside the gate, starting rusty in the woods but showing signs of use by the sentry boxes, where there was a wooden platform.

This time, I wasn't afraid of anyone. As soon as possible, I had to find out everything, go everywhere. But not with Viive.

We stood and stood in the breakfast line. My legs were getting tired. Everybody here was Estonian – lots of women and children and a few men. The children were standing in line for the adults, who sat on near-by benches, talking. Grown-ups were always talking, talking endlessly!

'Are we allowed outside the camp?' I asked Viive, as though I didn't really care.

'No, we are not.'

'Then what about those boys over there in the woods?' I had watched the boys for some time. They seemed to be searching for something. I saw them digging with pointed sticks in the ground.

'If the guards see them,' said Viive, 'they'll be shot.'

'Oh, yes?' But I knew she was lying. I knew the guards must have seen them a dozen times. They were right out in the open. It meant we could go out if we wanted to. And I meant to, at the first opportunity. I could see that Viive was growing up to be a 'young lady'. I knew the signs. She would tell lies to save her own skin. And mothers believed her type every time. Doing anything with her would be risky.

The line moved like a caterpillar with a thousand legs. We entered a kitchen, a big concrete room full of steam. Huge cooking pots were lined up on one side, with sweating, red-faced women behind each one. 'Next!' they kept shouting.

Viive gave me a prod, and I hurried towards one of them to pass her my bucket. 'One or two?' she asked.

'Say two,' Viive prompted me with another prod.

As if I didn't know it was two! 'Two, please.'

The woman poured out two ladlefuls of white stuff into the bucket, told me to take two pieces of bread, and I was through.

'You didn't have to prod me,' I told Viive.

'You're stupid!' she said.

'Do they have school here?'

'No.'

'You're stupid too,' I said to Viive, to get the last word.

When we got back to Memme, I felt good. No school! And I told her I liked this camp. At the same time I smiled at Viive's aunt. Next time I would ask her when they were leaving.

We sat on our beds and ate breakfast. The bundles had all

been shoved out of sight, and I felt that we belonged. People had drawn chairs close to our corner, or to be by the stove, and included us in their circle.

The white stuff was called 'rice', and the delicious dark things in the bottom were 'raisins'.

After breakfast there wasn't much to do. Some people went to take naps. The baby in the room started to cry again.

Memme said she had to do some mending, but Viive's aunt wanted to talk. So they talked. It was grown-up talk, and most of the sentences began with 'Do you remember?' or 'Whatever happened to ...?' It reminded me of when Unki had met Leena's father, and how I had never got close to Leena. I had wanted to so much and had overlooked Inge, who had turned out to be the best friend of all.

Viive said she was going out to play. I said I didn't want to. As soon as she was gone, I hurried outside and worked my way around the barracks, till I found an open spot in the barbed-wire fence. It was what I had been looking for, ideally hidden by a clump of bushes with none of the windows facing that way. The area looked well used and trampled, and was close to an odd-looking concrete-covered excavation that looked like a swimming pool, but was shallower and empty.

Making sure Viive wasn't anywhere around, I climbed over the wire and stepped into the woods. What a smell! It was even worse than by the latrines! What a stinky camp this was!

The ground was freshly turned and so soft that my boots sank down almost to the laces. Holding my nose, I waded on through. The trees weren't as thick as they looked from the camp side. There was sky ahead and open green.

But the smell was just awful! All this decay was like putting your finger in a rotten apple. Stepping from one bit of harder turf to another, I noticed a flash of metal in the mud. Silver buttons. What luck! But as I tried to pick them up, I realized they were still attached to a jacket. The jacket was deeply embedded in the soil. I pulled and pulled, but I couldn't budge it. The jacket was too deeply buried. Using Unki's knife, I cut the buttons off and looked around for more. These were German uniform buttons with the German eagle. Officer's buttons at least!

While I searched around for more buttons, I found some strange things. Two stones turned out to be moss-covered helmets; a vine-choked branch, an old rifle. As I tried to untangle the rifle, I noticed an old boot sticking out of the ground. With a stick I poked at the sock part, which looked funny. The stick went right through and that awful smell rose again, only worse than ever. It was like bursting a puffball. I threw up my rice-and-raisin breakfast all over the boot. Then I started running back to camp, back to Memme. There was something awful out there in the woods; I didn't know what. I had heard there were dead bodies buried in those fields, but I didn't know whether to believe it or not.

At the wire fence, I stopped for breath. What a ninny I was! Running like that from a bad smell! Inge wouldn't have run. She would have gone on to see what was at the other side of the woods.

Just then a plane flew over the camp. It was going to land somewhere nearby, and I wanted to see where. I turned around again and ran back through the woods, this time without stopping, keeping my eyes on the bright sky ahead.

I was glad I had changed my mind. Once I was out of the wood, the smell disappeared. There was a sunny pleasure of secret places in the fields, which were unploughed and banked against the sky. In the tall grass and dandelions, spring-fresh green and buttercup yellow, I found a special place again. To the left was a road flanked by a rolling, rising hillside. There were little hedges and summer-dry sticks and some straw, left lying after a past harvest.

To the right, the woods marched on into a pine forest. Should I turn left or right?

I decided to turn right today. I'd explore the left side tomorrow.

I'd hardly got beyond the first field when I recognized the railway tracks that passed the main gate. Here, too, they were rusty and overgrown. It meant that the trains came only as far as the camp gate.

I pretended I was a train, whistling through the night. 'Wheee-oosh!' Thundering through a station. The station master groped for his watch and checked it against the station clock. 'One minute late,' he grumbled. Brazil was this way. England was the other way, to the right, between the buttercups and dandelions, towards the pine woods. I stopped the engine for a minute to pick up a consignment of white bread from the American Zone. The passengers wouldn't ride this train unless they were served white bread. It was a secret sign. Rye bread meant they were on a Russian train and had to escape.

The train was going slow. People were sitting comfortably or looking out of the windows. Men were reading and women were talking. Birds were chirping and flying back and forth between the railway sleepers.

Suddenly I heard a plane. Air raid! The passengers started screaming. The train stopped, the lights went out. 'Into the ditch!' I yelled and jumped, rolling over and over down the slope into the pine needles. And I was laughing because it was just a game now. But the plane was real. It was coming straight down, so low I could see the pattern on its tyres. With my hands over my ears, I watched it fly over and then started running to see where it had landed.

Stumbling through the thick pine needles, I arrived at yet another embankment. I scrambled through thick blackberry vines and up the slope, to lie on my stomach in the long grass, panting as I caught my breath.

I watched the plane taxiing down a short runway, turning until it came to a full stop beside a row of other planes. I counted eight planes in all. A British flag flew over a corrugated-iron barracks, and soldiers were moving about the planes and the barracks, talking and smoking, laughing or just sitting on boxes having a cup of tea. I had heard that English tea was different from that of other people, and one day soon I was going to try some.

The pilot climbed out of the cockpit, head and shoulders first, removing his helmet. He waved to one of the men on the ground, then looked straight at me. Of course he couldn't see me, but I pressed myself into the ground anyway to wait for the challenge. None came. The men's voices didn't change in tone.

That had been a close one! I rolled back down the slope and returned to the safety of the pine woods, to the railway track, and the long grass on the camp side. I resolved to come here every day, to watch the planes land and take off.

Stuffing my cap into my jacket sleeve, I rolled in the grass a bit more. Then I decided to go back. What if Memme had 'got word', and we were moving again? And she couldn't find me? So I hurried back. At the barbed-wire fence I had barely got across when I spotted Viive by the pump.

'Where have you been?' she asked suspiciously, staring at my muddy boots.

'Oh, just around and about.'

'That isn't camp mud,' said Viive triumphantly. 'I'm going to tell your grandmother you've been outside the camp.'

'Go and tell!'

'Better still, I'm going to tell the guards. They'll shoot you,' said Viive, and turned towards the guard huts, smiling over her shoulder. 'Watch me go.'

'I don't care,' I called after her, and waved my hand in disgust. But you could never be too careful. Rather than call her bluff, I hurried over to the pump and washed my boots. When they were completely clean I went to the men's latrines, found the freshest and deepest mud, and waded around in it till my boots were dirty again, this time with camp mud.

Then I set off to look for Memme.

I found her still sitting by the stove talking. I went and stood beside her to wait for Viive and the guards.

They didn't come. Instead, I noticed the women all looking at me strangely. Memme stopped talking, sniffed the air, and led me aside. 'You haven't done a poo-poo in your pants, have you?' she asked.

I had not.

Nevertheless, she sniffed me all over and arrived at the conclusion that the smell was coming from my boots. From the latrines. The other women agreed this was a 'filthy' camp. Memme removed the boots and put them outside the door, 'to be cleaned later'.

Without shoes, I couldn't go outside. So I went to lie on my bed with one of my English books to learn English. Better late than never.

After a week and endless standing in line trying to be last because 'the nourishment is at the bottom', said Memme, I just couldn't stand it anymore. Viive was everywhere! The baby was always yelling! I wished his mother wouldn't dry his rags by our stove. But when he smiled, he was nicer. In the mornings sometimes, he said, 'Rrrrrr! Gagagaga!' and made soft gurgling noises.

I vowed that when I grew up, I wouldn't have babies. I was just going to have birds and fairies. Something quiet.

Memme was teaching me to knit with four needles, and I had started with a pair of gloves. The women commented on what a good girl I was, 'just like Viive', who was knitting too. With my eyes on the needles, I let my head be patted, if that was what they wanted to do.

One day they got the 'word', Viive and her aunt were to leave for England right after breakfast. I was going to be alone at last.

They left.

Dumping my knitting in a corner, I yelled to Memme from the door, 'I'm going out to play'. Straight through the wire and into the woods I went. Holding my nose against the stink, I arrived once more in freedom, a little surprised to find my special place was still there, unchanged – perhaps even a little greener and warmer; it was closer to summer.

I took the road to the left this time.

The excitement of adventure made me think of Unki. A real traveller had to have a walking stick and a knapsack. I cut myself a walking stick. If only I had Unki's knapsack now, the canvas one he carried everywhere with him. And his flask, full of those nasty-tasting 'spirits'.

The road was wide and muddy. Looking back, I could see the camp gates and the sentry posts. I hoped the guards were looking the other way.

The fields that were unploughed looked abandoned. Tractors and farm implements had been left to rust in the stubble. On closer inspection, I noticed they were not farm machinery at all but army trucks and jeeps and things. Most of the wheels were missing, but the steering wheels were still intact. This traveller was going to travel by car.

I climbed into the nearest jeep, sat behind the wheel, and asked everybody where they were going. 'Hold on,' I shouted. 'We're off!' The tooter didn't work. You couldn't drive a car without a tooter.

In the next car the seat was full of broken glass. So I went back to the one with the broken tooter and made my own horn go 'Brrr-toot-toot!' It had a good sound to it. It was an American car. Unki had told me that American cars were best, like American bread. Brrr-toot-toot, we were in Indochina. Brrr-toot-toot, and there was Brazil coming up on the right. Now for England. Mother was standing at the station, looking at her watch. But she was waiting for a train, not a car. I turned the wheel from side to side until I tired of that game.

Climbing onto the roof I tried to see as far as I could. Shading my eyes like a captain on a ship, I saw land ahead and also the camp, quite clearly. The road continued for a while, then turned suddenly uphill. Even on tiptoe I couldn't see across the rise. So I decided to go scouting around. The 'enemy' could be out there, I figured, or the guards wouldn't be carrying rifles. The thought didn't comfort me, so I decided to forget it. What enemy? Not the 'allies', as Unki called them. Though he hadn't explained who these 'allies' were. Another army, probably.

I climbed down to resume my journey. Taking big strides, of course. Travellers always took big strides. The road was intriguing because I could hear a funny thumping sound across the hill. A definite thumping. As I got nearer to the summit, it became steadily louder, like a whole army on the move. It had to be the 'allies'.

I reached the summit and stopped openmouthed. It *was* a whole army on the move, and it was coming straight towards me! The first soldier was only a few feet away. They were dressed for battle, with helmets and rifles, and those great big boots thumping the ground.

Without another thought I turned and ran.

Then I heard an order. The thumping had stopped. I stopped too and looked to see what had happened. To my horror, they were fixing bayonets. 'Charge!' The whole regiment was thundering after me.

I had never run so fast in my life or been so scared, not in Berlin or Hausberge or anywhere. Every time I turned I saw they were still coming until I didn't need to look anymore, the ground was shaking so.

I couldn't find my path to the woods. 'Memme!' I had to get back to the camp, and the quickest way was through the gate and past the sentries.

I ran blindly, falling and running again. There was a stitch in my side, my throat was tight, and my chest hurt. My knees were giving. The road was starting to waver from side to side. But still they were after me. The sentries had seen us coming and had come out into the road to watch. Crying now, I called for help, but they just stood there waiting – waiting for me to be caught. Or waiting to shoot me themselves! Viive had been telling the truth after all. They were going to shoot me.

It was all too much! I threw myself down at the side of the road to await the worst. Another order rang out. I knew it would be 'Shoot'. The column halted. I buried my face in the soil and lay still. Maybe they would think I was dead already.

But the shot didn't come.

The ground started shaking again. I lifted my head, slowly at first, and what do you know, the column was still charging. Only this time in the other direction, back up the hill, the way they had come.

At the same time I heard a loud hoot of laughter from the camp gate. I wiped my eyes. The sentries were doubled up, yelping and holding their stomachs. One waved to me weakly before collapsing again into another spasm of laughter.

'*Kurat!*' I said. Which was the strongest Estonian word that I knew. The soldiers hadn't been chasing me at all. They had been training.

I wiped my suit and the dust off my hat before pulling it low over my eyes.

'Hey, you there!'

I gritted my teeth. The worst part was yet to come. I couldn't go around now to the fence, and so had to pass those stupid guards. Just as well Viive wasn't around anymore. She'd die if she heard this one.

The guards were still laughing when I sauntered up to them. One of them pulled me under the barrier by my braid. He tried to look at me, but I wouldn't look back. I kept my eyes on his boots while he talked. His voice was friendly enough. Another knelt in front of me, spat on his handkerchief, and started wiping my face. When he was finished, he said, 'Watch it!' and got up.

They said other things, too, that I couldn't understand, and then pushed me towards the barracks.

Without looking back, I hurried to our room. Memme was sitting by the stove where I had left her, knitting my discarded glove. I put my arm around her and gave her a kiss.

Sitting on a stone behind our barracks in the dark, with a towel around my shoulders, Memme was going through my hair with a fine-tooth comb. Each pull through was followed by an 'Aih' and 'Oih' as shower after shower of wriggling lice fell into the mud.

We had been sitting there since after supper. I wanted to catch the lice and let them run along my arm, but Memme was in such a mood, I didn't want to try her.

To me it was all the same, as long as I could keep my hair. The women had been talking, saying the children should have their heads shaved. They had looked at me too, to which Memme replied that I was 'clean'. And that was why we had to come out in the dark.

'All right,' said Memme at last. She straightened her stiff spine. We changed places.

Memme tied the apron around her neck and started combing her own hair, inspecting the comb minutely between pulls. Then, suddenly, there was one! And another! So I sat on another stone to wait for her to finish too.

Most of the boys had had their heads shaved. It looked awful! And here I had been trying to grow my hair long enough for me to sit on it. When Mimma would meet us at that station in England she would say, 'My goodness! Look at those beautiful long braids!' My rattails would be forgotten. But if they cut my hair off . . .

‘We’re going back,’ Memme whispered. She tied the apron around her waist again and hid the comb in the pocket. With her pushing me in front, we groped our way to bed.

But the bugs were getting to everybody, the same as in the last camp. People were packing their things together, spreading them on the floor, and sleeping on their bundles instead of on the beds. Then, suddenly, word went around, and everybody started racing for floor space. Memme grabbed our bundles from under the bed and threw them back in the old corner by the stove. Just in time! An hour later there wasn’t enough room left to put a foot down. The straw sacks were thrown outside. People were angry, muttering and grumbling. They wanted to throw the beds out, too, but couldn’t move them, as they were nailed to the wall. So they tore out the boards for firewood and for building walls around the separate encampments.

There was no more chatting and knitting around the stove, only bitter arguments and dispute. Memme dared not leave the room anymore. She feared that our things would be moved while she was gone, that someone else would take our place.

In the other barracks it was the same. The men had moved out into the yard and were threatening to burn the camp down.

A few mornings later, the guards came to the door and told us to pack. We were herded together into the centre of the compound. Memme sat on a bench, exhausted. She didn’t look well. I held her hand while the guards went about counting and sorting families into groups.

Our group was led into another barracks in another section of the camp. These barracks hadn’t been used before.

We stepped into yet another long room, but this one was completely empty. There were no beds or bunks, just a stove in one corner. Memme, without hesitation, made straight for the stove.

There were some funny-looking wash lines drawn from wall to wall. Memme showed me that they were for hanging up blankets to form walls. 'We'll close up the three sides. Leave the fourth for later.' Because of the stove.

All over the room, blanket walls were rising around each family. Another rope built an aisle down the centre of the room. I thought it was the most exciting place I had ever lived in. In a blanket house, in a blanket town, with a blanket main street!

Memme wasn't so glad except that at last she could change her underwear in privacy. And she made me change too. By closing our 'front door' with the quilt blanket, we shut out everybody and everything. It was just me and Memme alone. I liked it so much that I didn't even want to go out to play. Instead, I watched Memme cutting her toenails. She heated some water first, to soak them, so she wouldn't break the scissors. We only had one pair of scissors.

I went out briefly to get our food. Then we sat together again in the warmth of the stove, in our underwear. Memme cut her nails, then did the washing, hanging it over the stove side of the blanket line. She washed herself and she washed me too. And then we dried our hair. Memme had such beautiful hair, grey and long, right down to her waist. I wished she would wear it loose instead of in a bun. If I had hair that long, I would never wear a bun.

I liked this blanket room so much I wished we could stay here forever. I liked rolling on the soft bundles and talking in whispers, with Memme and no one else. And no one else could see us. With all my disappointments, I realized that Memme was the only one who had remained constant. Of all the people in the world, she had never let me down.

In this camp, I had heard talk about 'bodies' out in the woods, about a 'mass grave' covered with cement. Memme drew me away and said to pay no heed. 'Just talk,' she said. But I wouldn't go to the latrine alone at night. Memme had to come with me.

After supper, Memme fixed the blankets on all sides and we

lay down to sleep. But whichever way Memme faced, her feet stuck out outside the wall. She sighed and left them that way. The lights went out.

I hadn't noticed much noise while we had been up and talking. But when we were lying down, other people's whispers seemed louder. It was strange to hear men's voices in the room. I bet Unki was in Brazil by now, halfway up the coffee mountains.

Memme was sleeping soundly.

I wondered what other people were doing. Were they lying down like us or sitting up? I wondered what they were wearing. The more I thought about them, the more I wanted to see if they were different from us. Or the same. Or what.

The feeling became so strong, it made me shift around until I was on the floor and lifting a corner of our blanket to peer down the 'road'. It was empty, but some of the 'walls' had mysterious bulges to them and some were moving. There were voices – some low, some loud. There was laughing and whispering. A baby was crying, probably the same one that had been in the other barracks.

My fingers itched to lift the blanket across from ours, just a little corner. It was so still in there. I inched forward and let my two fingers raise the barrier just a teeny bit. An old lady was sleeping on her back, mouth open. She was fully dressed, like us. It was comforting.

'What are you doing?' asked Memme angrily, with a hand on the seat of my trousers. She hauled me back to our 'room' and started giving me a lecture. The lecture was so long that I fell asleep.

20 Memme is Lost!

'Take your fingers out of the soup,' said Memme. 'And go and wash your face and hands.'

'Are we going to England now?'

'No, to another transit camp.'

I told Memme I didn't want any more soup, and dragged my towel to the pump for the last time. I counted to twenty, dashed into the latrine, and out again. It looked as if we would never get to England.

I had lost count of time in this camp. But time was funny. Sometimes it was long and boring, other times exciting and short. I hardly knew where it went. But the longest time in the world was clock time. Ever tried counting a minute? It lasts for an hour, at least. And five minutes – I couldn't stand it! For instance, when Memme took my temperature, our thermometer had to be charged up for five minutes under my armpit. Five full minutes! A whole day went by before it was ready.

But if I didn't count time, it went by like a flash. And it was always the good time that was short. I had come to the conclusion that there wasn't any time anyway. Time was something the grown-ups had invented for themselves, so they would have something to watch and wait for. They couldn't live without it. 'What time is it?' they were always asking.

And school needed time so everybody would arrive and leave together. People had clocks so they could meet each other and both turn up at the same time. Leena always ate at six. Every time it was six o'clock, I knew Leena would be eating. But they were talking about clock time, and if it weren't for meeting and going places together, we wouldn't need it. There was no need to eat at six. We often ate at five or ten past or just when Memme was ready and said I had to eat.

Sitting on a bench in the middle of the camp and listening to the women talking about time, I wondered, Why bother? One woman said she fed her baby at seven; another, at eight; a third one, at ten minutes to nine.

One woman came and said she was only staying for a 'few minutes' and stayed all morning. Another went away for 'a minute' and didn't come back at all.

I had been carving Memme a wooden spoon with Unki's penknife. Not a big spoon. Just a little spoon. I wanted to finish it.

And now suddenly time had run out again and there were things left unfinished. I wanted to go to the airport one last time, to say good-bye to it. And to the fields and woods around it. And to the pilots, too, though they didn't know I existed.

I wondered what time it was now.

We had to be at the station at seven thirty.

I dared not risk it. The sun was already getting warmer and the woods less dark and mysterious.

Why did the morning sun always make things brighter and more colourful than during the day?

Memme ran her hand down the towel and said I hadn't washed properly. There wasn't time to send me back. The soldiers were coming to the door. We were leaving.

Memme and I carried the bundles to the gate. I carried my pink blanket bundle and the food basket. There were so many people, I had trouble keeping Memme in sight. The basket was awkward and grazed against my leg.

At the gate, a whistle blew. The red-and-white barrier was raised and we were ordered to move forward, to form a row along the platform: I was right. The trains did only come to the gate and no farther.

The soldiers were moving among us, pushing and dividing us into groups. They seemed to be in a hurry and impatient. 'You, over there,' shouted a soldier to someone. But the man wanted to go the other way to be with his relatives.

I clung to Memme's coat. There was so much moving about I was afraid of being pushed onto the rails. The train was coming. A big monstrous engine was hissing and steaming towards the platform. As it approached, it towered above us, so that even the wheels were taller than the tallest man. I knew why it was so big. We were on ground level, that was why. Usually platforms were built higher, and then trains looked smaller.

The engine ground to a halt. It was pulling cattle wagons with big doors. The soldiers opened the doors and we were told to climb inside.

Memme made for the nearest opening and started throwing our bundles through the door. She hoisted me up after them and told me to pack them into a corner. I did as I was told. I liked corners.

Memme herself was helped up by a guard, who said 'Upsy-daisy' as he gave her a boost with his arm. I liked the sound of that word. 'Upsy-daisy,' I repeated to myself, so I would remember it. And I kept on repeating it under my breath.

'What did you say?' Memme asked. She was short of breath and started looking for her pills.

People were pressing in on us from all sides. The doors were slammed shut. We were left in the dark, close up against each other. I reached for Memme's hand and held it tightly.

But it wasn't really so dark once our eyes got used to it. There were a number of wire-covered air vents close to the ceiling. Everybody was trying to reach those vents. One woman was screaming that she couldn't breathe, another that she was fainting. Memme let go of my hand so she could take her tablets.

'Open the doors,' someone shouted from the back.

The train was moving fast, shaking and swaying from side to

side. The old rails hadn't seen much use lately, and there was a lot of screeching on rust and scraping of metal.

It was getting hot. Memme removed my jacket and opened her coat. She was gasping for air and told me to hold my head up. 'Breathe slowly,' she instructed me.

But the men had already started working on the door. With a clatter of chains and bolts, the huge iron door slid open. Fresh air and sunshine filled the boxcar.

Because of all the shoving and pushing towards the air vents, Memme and I found ourselves in the middle of the car, right by the open door. Memme forced me down quickly, with my legs dangling over the edge. She herself sat right behind me, holding the back of my pants. Soon there were so many people wedged beside me into the doorway that I couldn't have fallen out if I had wanted to.

The wind was fresh in my face, blowing my hair. There were cows on the German farms. The train whistled past and they barely lifted their heads. Families were out in the fields, ploughing. They didn't even look up, although a few children waved, and I waved back. The countryside had changed since the bombs had stopped falling. It looked lived in again.

But the towns and the cities were the same. I had almost forgotten. The bigger cities were all in ruins, forming their own countryside of a forest of blackened chimneys with the sky showing through.

As the train slowed down through a line of railway workers who were mending the rails, people stopped chattering and moved forward in the boxcar to stare grimly at the rubble and ruins. Memme put a firm arm around my waist and whispered bitterly, 'Look, child, and remember. This was war.'

Soon the sun was travelling much lower beside us. No longer was it just a light, but a round bouncing ball rebounding on the trees and meadows, dipping into lakes and rivers, and running along the horizon, playing hide and seek.

'I'm thirsty.'

Memme put her hand on my head to comfort me. 'It won't be long now. We're almost there.' She sighed. I leaned back on her chest and closed my eyes, letting the golden light dance on my eyelids. The wheels were going clickety-click, clickety-click.

Memme was shaking me gently to wake up. 'We're stopping,' she said.

The train was on a bridge and entering a huge station. All the glass was broken, but the frame was still standing. I rubbed my eyes and looked down through the girders at roadworks. Cranes and trucks were parked beside piles of brick and lumber. New houses were being built amid the ruins, and a few street lights were on, though it wasn't dark yet.

A lot of people were at the station.

The train pulled into a platform. The soldiers came back and started grouping us once more. Memme said we had to change trains. She piled our bundles on the platform into a big mound and told me to sit on top of it. I was not to move, she warned me. She herself had to go somewhere, she said, and disappeared into the crowd.

I climbed on top of the bundles and watched the people milling around me. One woman was calling, 'Arno, where are you?' Another was saying, 'Father, can't you hurry up!' A voice called, 'Salme, where is Salme?' in a panic. And 'My brown suitcase is missing. God! Where is my brown suitcase?'

I wondered if all these people were going to England too. It was only a matter of time, Memme had said. Then we three would start life all over again. I looked forward to the boat ride. Memme had said there would be a boat ride and that we were on our way to Holland.

The platform was narrow and so full that sometimes I thought someone was going to fall over the edge. The boxcars moved out. The space between the platforms became empty. There were just as many people on the other side. Many of them started crossing over to our side, and I wondered if we had to move too. I wished Memme were back.

As the two platforms mingled, I could hear Latvian, Ukrainian, and Russian, and less and less Estonian.

I tried to see which way Memme had gone, but all I could make out was a big broken station clock. And strangers.

If only she would hurry!

A new train was approaching. Those still on the rails clambered up the other side. I had a feeling we should have crossed maybe.

This one was a passenger train. As soon as it had stopped, the soldiers started pushing and directing. Our bundles got knocked sideways. I rebuilt them quickly and climbed up again to wave to Memme when she came. Where was she? The soldiers were telling us to get into the train. They had a big iron chain and had divided the platform into two sections. Those on the other side of the chain had to wait. But the others must 'Hurry, hurry!'

'Memme!' I called in panic.

'Memme!' I screamed across the chain.

One of the soldiers saw me and lifted me up with one arm.

'No, no!' I protested. I struggled and fought, but he didn't even flinch. He was carrying me to the train window.

As the doors were all blocked, he hoisted me up through the window into a pair of strange arms. The arms responded and pulled me through. I found myself sitting on a strange woman's lap. The woman was smiling and shaking her head. 'Tsk, tsk!' she was saying at my tears. She was Russian.

'Babushka! Babushka!' I yelled past her out of the window, trying to explain, and pointing my finger towards the platform. But she thought I was calling *her* Babushka. She was pleased and pressed me closer as the carriage filled to capacity. No amount of struggling could make her understand what I wanted. I slipped down at last between her knees, under the train seat. But there was no way out from there either. Bundles, baskets, hems, and feet blocked me at every turn.

When at last I managed to raise my head again and look out of the train window, I saw that the platform this side of the chain was empty except for the soldiers. The train doors were being banged shut.

'Memme,' I screamed for the last time, but hopelessly.

A whistle blew, and the train started pulling out. Memme! Memme! My only Memme!

I climbed back under the seat to lie on the wooden floor. I couldn't live without Memme. She was the only one I loved. She was my world! And now I was alone. I started to cry. It had happened so suddenly, so unexpectedly, that I didn't know what to do.

The Russian woman kept putting her head under the seat to see if I was all right. 'Tsk, tsk,' she kept repeating over and over and over.

The floor was hard but warm. The wheels were no longer jumping clickety-click, but were calling 'Memme ... Memme ...' under my cheek.

When Memme had stuck some of her own hair on my doll's head, I hadn't been grateful. And I had never finished knitting that glove. Now I would never be able to tell her how much I loved her. I couldn't remember if I ever did tell her. I would never be able to tell her that I was glad she never got angry at me when I came home wet or late. She had kept me safe from the bombs. She had held my hand all night ...

Strong arms lifted me from under the seat. The Russian woman was being kind. She pushed the matted hair out of my eyes, talking all the time. She was telling me a story. Leena's babushka used to tell the same one, about a stove that travelled all over the world and had adventures. I listened, understanding a word here and there, but my eyes were heavy, and it was another voice in my mind that was talking. In my mind, Memme was standing on the platform, waving good-bye as the train started to move out. She said she was going to Brazil, too, to join Unki, that she had to live her 'own life' too. I wanted to ask her to take me with her, but she was strange and distant, smiling and waving but, like Unki, shaking her head. And suddenly, I saw a flock of birds flying over the station. They were swans but with people's heads. Among them I saw my mother and my father, Tätä and my other grandmother, and wait... There was Inge.

I woke up sharply. The train had stopped. We were in another station. Strong lights were on everywhere. We had stopped alongside some tall, tall houses. They were the tallest houses I had ever seen, at least six storeys high. These must be the 'sky-scrapers', which Unki had told me about. Maybe we were in America.

There was a great bustle to get out of the train. The Russian woman set me down and straightened my jacket. She looked inside my hat for something, then placed it on my head, the wrong way around. She wanted me to wait. I wasn't waiting for anyone. I had to find Memme. She was probably in another part of the train.

I climbed over the baskets and placed myself in the outgoing stream of traffic which was flowing towards the doors. Clinging to a woman's flowered cotton dress and a wicker suitcase, I was pushed along until I stood free once more, on the edge of the platform.

There was that familiar red-and-white-striped barrier at the end, and guards with rifles. The barrier was open and the soldiers were directing us through, across the tracks, and towards those big buildings.

I ran ahead as fast as I could, and stood next to one of the soldiers. I could watch the people's faces from there, looking for the one and only face in the world with a hat on top and a matted silver-fox collar.

The soldier soon noticed me. 'Come on!' he said, giving me a gentle push forward. 'Let's go!'

'No, no!' I protested, vigorously shaking my head to make him understand. 'No! No! No!'

He saw that something was wrong. He put his rifle against the sentry post and knelt down. He was so tall! His face was friendly, but he was speaking English and I didn't understand more than a word or two.

'Memme.' I pointed into the passing crowd. All the English words I knew had gone clean out of my mind.

'Your mother?' he asked finally.

'Yes, mother,' which was as good as grandmother.

'Come with me.' He stood up again, put a hand on my shoulder, and pushed me across the tracks to one of the guards.

The guard tried to speak to me too but ended up shouting. Slowly and loudly he repeated the words over and over. Apparently he thought I was deaf. But the trouble wasn't in the sound. It was the words themselves I didn't understand.

A third soldier was called.

They patted him on the shoulder. 'Speak Deutsch,' they assured me. So I told him my tale from the beginning, how I had been piling the bundles up neatly and sitting on them waiting for Memme when the soldiers with the chain separated the platform. 'Now I'll never see my Memme again.'

The soldier listened intently but was puzzled. When I finished he reached into his pocket and produced a tiny dictionary. He leafed through it for the words he wanted. '*Grossmutter . . . anderen.*' More leafing. '*Zug*' he told me, patting my cheek to say it was all right. Memme was on the next train or another train.

With his hand on my head he led me back to the platform. And, sure enough, another train was stopping. The doors were opened. People stumbled out in the same chaos and milled past us. I watched each face desperately. I craned my head, and the soldier looked too. That one? Not that one. This one? No.

A hat looked familiar! Memme, Memme! I rushed into the crowd and grasped an arm. A stranger looked down, surprised and a little annoyed. 'Have you seen my grandmother?' I asked in Estonian. The woman didn't understand and shook me loose.

Running from one to another, I tried both Estonian and German. Everybody was in a hurry. No, haven't seen. Who?

'Well?' asked the soldier.

I shook my head. The platform was almost empty. The last people were going by, a woman with two children. Tears started falling again.

'There, there,' said the soldier and took my hand. We returned to the guard post. The soldier shrugged his shoulders. No one knew what to do. It was getting very dark beyond the bright lights.

My dictionary friend pressed my fingers reassuringly and said, 'Come on'. We went through the barrier and into the camp, towards the buildings. They had at least a hundred windows each. The road was unpaved and muddy. The houses smelled of wet concrete and seemed to be covered with a sweaty type of cold. I had to put my head back to see the top storey. I had liked the wooden barracks better. They had been so cosy and warm.

All the windows were brightly lighted. The streetlamps had a cold electric light that made us all look greenish in the face. I looked at my friend. He looked down at me. He was a funny man. He took my hat and tried it on his own head. It almost fit him too. 'Look,' he said, and wiggled his ears, first one, then the other, then both together. Unki used to be able to do that.

I asked if he could wiggle his nose and lift one eyebrow without moving the other. He could do that too.

After leafing through the dictionary again he came up with the word *Sohn.* He levelled his hand to his belt, about so high. '*Mein Sohn John.*' He had a son called John.

I nodded to show that I understood. I was actually surprised that they do have people called John, Henry, Mary, and Jane in England. Some of the English sounds didn't seem so strange anymore.

We reached a wooden hut, some kind of office. The British flag was flying outside, and a sign on the door had some writing on it. The soldier rapped on the door smartly, then stopped to wait.

A voice boomed, 'Come in'. We stepped over the threshold. My friend saluted, very precise and military now. No more ear wiggling. After a few brief words back and forth, I was pushed towards the desk and the grey-haired officer sitting behind it. A bare electric bulb hung above his head. It occurred to me to salute too, but the officer's face said, No nonsense. He was probably a general.

There was more talkety-talk, which ended with the general's putting his elbows on the desk, placing his fingertips together, and looking straight at me. 'Something, something, name?'

I told him my name.

'No, no,' he said sharply.

'*Grossmutter* name,' whispered the soldier into my ear.

And then I had this awful moment. I didn't know Memme's name the way he wanted it. It was Mrs Something, but was hardly ever used where I had reason to hear it. We went by my mother's name, and in Estonian, she was called *armuline proua*, which is a formal way of address among strangers. Of course I knew it, but the officer's face was fierce and impatient. His sternness didn't help me to think straight.

'Memme,' I said hesitatingly, but knew it was not what he wanted.

The soldier and general looked at each other and shrugged. The general raised his eyebrows in an exasperated way and started sifting through his papers. But after a minute he threw them aside and gave an order.

The soldier said, 'Yes, sir!' saluted again, and pushed me ahead of him out of the office.

Once outside, he softened up again, and we looked at each other in the green light. What now? He wasn't going to leave me, was he? I held on to his sleeve, but he patted my head. 'All right!' He went on patting me absentmindedly while he looked around.

Then he had an idea. 'Eat,' he shrugged and rubbed his tummy.

I had forgotten all about food since I lost Memme. I was hungry, but I didn't want to eat. I wanted to find Memme first. So I shook my head – No.

Yet the soldier insisted. He led me around the buildings to a central block and pushed me through a big door, into a dining room. The meals had all been finished. The tables were stacked with dirty dishes, and bread crumbs littered the floor. Two women in white overalls were moving about clearing and cleaning.

I noticed there was a partly emptied plate of bread on every table. White bread! I wanted to sit at a table right away, but the soldier said No. We had to go through a metal barrier first, to a counter. There were other plates of bread, untouched. He took one, and only then did we go to sit at a table.

It was white bread, a whole plateful. And although it was nice to have a whole plate to myself, I couldn't help looking at all those other plates where the bread was being wasted. The women were actually wiping the bread into a bin and throwing it out.

The soldier motioned for me to begin eating.

I took a bite. And to my further delight, I discovered it wasn't just bread. There was a thick layer of strawberry jam between the two pieces. The soldier laughed when I licked the jam with my tongue and nibbled at the bread, which was like cake. Imagine, I thought, eating so much cake at one time! But the English must eat this way every day.

The table clearers were coming closer. I was afraid they

would take my plate away before I had finished. At the same time, I couldn't eat any faster. My mouth was full, and I was thinking of tucking a few pieces in my jacket for later, wondering if the soldier would mind my doing that.

He wasn't eating and seemed amused.

When my plate was empty at last, I couldn't help looking at those other plates again. Imagine throwing all that food away! The soldier followed my glance and, with a long reach of his arm, brought one of the half-empty plates to our table, right from under the cleaning woman's nose.

I decided, never mind manners! I was going to fill myself to the brim with this bread and jam. There was no way of knowing when I might eat again or find anything this good.

But my eyes were bigger than my stomach. My eyes wanted more, but my stomach was full, and my teeth were tired. There were still five sandwiches left. I knew that if I left them, I would think about them later. Tomorrow, when I had nothing to eat, I would remember them and regret having left them.

The soldier saw me slowing down and thought I was through. 'O.K.,' he asked. He was about to rise.

'O.K.' I rose too but with a sideways movement. A slip of the hand and five pieces of bread were safely tucked inside my jacket. The soldier hadn't noticed. At least he didn't say anything.

Now that my stomach was full and there was enough for later, I realized with shame that I hadn't thought about Memme once during that meal. My heart started to ache again.

We entered one of the huge buildings, but everything was quiet. The long corridor was empty, and the doors were all closed. The soldier looked at his watch. 'Too late,' he said and showed me. It was half past eleven.

'*Morgen.*' He put his hands under his head. 'Now sleep. O.K.?'

'No sleep. Memme.'

'*Morgen.*'

'No, no. *Heute*.'

The soldier scratched his head perplexed, showed me his watch again, then did some rifle drills and said, 'Me, sleep. *Morgen, Grossmutter*.'

He wanted to sleep so he could go on duty early in the morning. And then we would look for Memme.

I wanted to look for her today. '*Nein, heute*,' I argued.

But the soldier had made up his mind. He spread his arms hopelessly and started walking towards the barracks.

I ran back to the building. The corridor was just as empty and the doors closed, but there were six corridors. I ran up the stairs to each one in the hope that someone was still up, that a door would be open and I could talk to someone, but I was out of luck. It was all so quiet that I wondered if the building wasn't empty.

So I hurried to the next one. This one was packed with people, all sitting on their belongings and trying to sleep propped up against the wall. The rooms hadn't been shared out yet. Searching through all six corridors, I still didn't find Memme, and no one spoke Estonian. 'You have to find the Estonian house,' a man told me in German.

But the third building was as quiet as the first one. Dare I knock on a door? I wondered. Then at least I would know if I was in the right house. I hesitated before the first door and knocked ever so softly. There was a sound of bedsprings, shuffling, and a face appeared at the partially opened crack. On seeing me, he slammed the door shut again. From the swearing and grumbling that followed, I knew they were Lithuanians. At least I was getting closer.

With renewed hope, I tried all six corridors, shouting Memme as I ran along each one. A few doors were opened and slammed shut again. People were angry. The soldier had been right. It was late.

The Estonians had to be in the fourth house.

Outside again, I sat on the steps to think of what to do. I could sleep right here in the corridor, or I could go on to try one more house. My clothes were dusty from sitting on the steps, and when I reached into my jacket for the bread and jam, I found I couldn't face it. So I threw it away and decided to go on searching.

The fourth building was quiet too. No one answered my first knock. So I tried another door. A faint '*Ja?*' made my heart leap with joy. Estonians! Memme had to be right there somewhere, probably sitting by a window waiting for me.

'Memme, Memme!' I screamed along the corridors once more. Up and down the stairs I ran, until one of the doors was opened, and a woman in a nightgown asked me what was wrong. Why wasn't I in bed? Her hair was twisted into some kind of paper bows or ties, and I couldn't help staring at them, while I told her what had happened, how I had lost my Memme.

She listened.

While I was telling the story, it all came back to me in detail and I started crying.

The lady turned much friendlier. She said that although she didn't know Memme personally, she had heard that someone was searching for a child. 'Go to the office in the morning. But right now, go to sleep,' she suggested, and yawned.

I said thank you and let her close the door. Then it occurred to me that I had forgotten to ask where . . . where was I supposed to sleep? I dared not knock again. The light under the door had gone out already.

There was something dismal and lonely about the big building, with everybody in a separate room. The corridors were so empty they made me feel unhappy twice over. I liked it best when people were close enough so you could touch them and see them. It was what I liked best about camp life.

I decided to return to that third building where people were still waiting for rooms. I would slip in beside them and sleep in the corridor, unnoticed and safe.

Between the chilly buildings, I thought I heard music and the sound of laughter and men's voices. The soldiers' barracks were still lighted up. The doors were open. A radio was playing dance music.

The light drew me forward. Perhaps I would find my friend again. I stopped just outside the circle of light. The room was full of soldiers. Some of them were playing cards around a huge green table, others were lying on their bunks, and a few were standing and smoking or watching the card players. Still others were by the open door. I daren't go closer. My friend wasn't there. But the guard I had spoken to was there, the one who had shouted instead of talking. He was at the other side of the room, lying on his bunk and reading a soft book with a colourful cover.

Suddenly, a heavy hand descended on my shoulder. I jumped with fright. 'What have we here?' asked the soldier, looking down at me. He must have come from the pump, because he was carrying a towel.

He called the others. All eyes turned in my direction as the soldier pushed me through the doorway.

The card players stopped between hands and stared at me over their card fans. The laughter trailed away, but the music blared on cheerfully as before.

'Come on in,' said one of the soldiers by the door. And he bowed deeply. 'Madam!'

I stood dumbly and debated whether to go closer or to run away. The hand was still on my shoulder. The soldiers seemed friendly. I searched out the eyes of the guard and saw to my delight that he recognized me. He closed his book and came to meet me. 'Hello, there!' he bellowed.

I rushed up to him and whispered into his ear. '*Grossmutter no.*'

He tweaked my nose playfully, shouted something to the others, and departed.

I was told to come in, to sit on the table. The card players shifted their chairs to make room. Someone lifted me up. Smiling broadly, the soldiers tried to speak to me with the only German words they knew, like '*schöne Fräulein, gehen Sie spazieren mit mir?*' (Pretty lady, will you take a walk with me?) '*Ich suche das ... der, die Toilette.*' (I am looking for the toilet.) '*Ich und du essen?*' (You and me eat?)

Each sentence was greeted with a hoot of derision or a quick stern 'Hush'; it wasn't suitable. Someone clapped his hands over my ears, but I liked it all a lot.

The guard returned. My friend was with him. He was only half dressed – in uniform trousers and a white cotton undershirt. He must have been sleeping, for he was rubbing his eyes and yawning.

'Hello!' he greeted me from the door. '*So Grossmutter no?*'

'No.' I shook my head negatively.

'O.K.' He patted my cheek. 'But now *schlafen.*'

'O.K.'

He lifted me off the table and piloted me through the room to the very end. He showed me an empty bunk and repeated, '*Schlafen.*' I was to sleep there.

The soldiers crowded around the bed nodding encouragement. One made a snoring sound to be sure there was no misunderstanding.

It was all right with me. I was a soldier too! If only Rein could see me now, and Inge!

My hat and boots were taken off and my boots placed under the bed. I lay down, and a thick army blanket was pulled up to my chin. The faces started leaving one by one. 'Good night!' I smiled at each man in turn and repeated 'Good night' as many times as I had to, until I found myself alone.

Funny how little you really needed to know of a language to get by! Come on. Come here. O.K. Hello!

The lights in my part of the room were turned off. It became nicely dark but not black dark. The bulb over the card table was still burning. The men returned to their game, to the music and smoking. Tomorrow we would find Memme.

I felt cosy and safe again. My eyes were heavy. The sandman had come. I wished he hadn't. I would rather have stayed awake and watched the card game, and talked to the soldiers.

The bulb hanging over the table took on a halo of light. It was like a sun in a distant place. Inside that light bulb, there was a sun. The table was a green meadow. I ran in the long grass. It was our garden in Estonia. There were Tondu and Memme. They were waiting for me on the side porch. What a surprise! They saw me and started running to meet me. Memme's arms opened to receive me. Tondu's tail was stiff and upright with happiness.

I ran and ran and the wind hindered me, I was going so fast. But at last I reached Memme and threw myself crying into her arms.

I was being shaken awake. My soldier friend was bending over the bed. Time to get up. It was light outside the window. My friend put a finger to his lips, not to make a noise. He handed me my boots and helped me lace them. I found my hat and was ready.

The room was full of sleeping soldiers, though some were getting up too, slowly. Stretching and scratching, grousing and grumbling.

My friend was still in his undershirt. He had a towel and soap and his jacket over his arm. '*Waschen,*' he said shortly.

On the way to the pump it all came back to me – Memme and everything – and also that while I had been in those tall buildings, I had seen some washrooms with rows of washbasins attached to the wall. And taps. And toilets. I had never seen such toilets before. Cubicles that you could lock from the inside. Porcelain toilet bowls, finer than Memme's best cups, with chains that released a whole waterfall of water gushing down into the floor – or wherever it went – gurgling all the way. And I would rather go and wash there instead of at the pump.

I put a little water in my hand and dabbed my face. My friend showed me how to gargle. He did it just like Unki used to, and washed himself by putting his whole head under the pump. He flicked the water off his hair and said, 'O.K. Finished?'

But not yet. He pulled a comb from his pocket. He combed his own hair, then hesitated. He fingered my matted braids, looked suspiciously into my parting, whistled, and said, 'Never mind!' He put the comb away.

'Now eat.'

Again? But I remembered last night's bread and jam with a desperate feeling of hunger. '*Brot?*'

He nodded.

How easy it was to speak English! No teacher had ever made it so easy.

We went back to the dining room. It was strange to remember this was still a camp. Instead of the food line I was used to and the half-dressed, uncombed, and any-old-how-as-long-as-you-had-a-place people, I saw that everyone was dressed up. All the people were neat and clean, and the line wasn't long. It moved quickly alongside the counter. First you took a tray. Then you chose your food. Did I want porridge or corn flakes, tea or coffee or milk? Real milk. The cutlery was at a separate table. It surprised me to see it lying around like that, with no one guarding it. And people, instead of taking it with them, actually left it behind when they had finished eating.

We took our tray to one of the tables. My friend wasn't eating again. He showed me his watch. '*Arbeit.*'

He had to go on duty.

'You eat,' he told me and patted my arm.

'But *Grossmutter?*' He wasn't going to forget, was he?

'*Grossmutter* later. Now *Arbeit*. Work.'

'O.K.'

He left me sitting in front of my porridge, milk, bread, and jam. I understood he had to work. He was a soldier and must obey orders. But I wished he didn't have to all the same.

All the tables were full of people eating and talking. It was like in a theatre, there was so much excitement and noise. All that was missing was Memme. What if I never found her again? These people might take me to England, but then I would have to explain to Mother that I had lost Memme on the way. She would never forgive me. I was supposed to take care of Memme. Unki's last words had been 'Take care of Memme'.

Breakfast over, I decided to go back to the Estonian building and, first, to visit one of those fabulous 'bathrooms'. That's what people called them, although I hadn't seen a bathtub in them.

The bathroom was full of women, mostly looking into the mirrors and doing their hair, and, of course, talking. I entered one of the cubicles, locked the door, and sat down. I ran my hand along the porcelain seat. It was smooth like a china cup. Even the floor and walls were made of china. It seemed a shame to go to the toilet here at all. There was a roll of paper hanging on the door, yards and yards of it. I wondered what it was for. Perhaps to write on while you were sitting and had some urgent thoughts? Or to send a message to the next cubicle if you got locked in?

I looked around for the box of 'bulletins' for wiping, but there weren't any. There were no rags or packing paper or anything. I didn't care, but I bet there were some people who would use the writing paper and waste it. I wouldn't, of course. But I could write a message for Memme, if I could find a pencil . . .

Then, suddenly, I heard her voice. I listened again, to be sure, but someone else was talking now. I must have imagined it.

No, wait, there it was again. It was! It was!

It was Memme!

With my pants still hanging around my knees, I stormed out of the cubicle, crying, 'Memme, Memme' and pushing everybody aside. I threw myself straight into her arms.

Memme was taken aback for a moment. Then her arms tightened around me, and I knew it was all right.

When I finally looked up at her, her face was stern.

'Where did you get to?' she asked. 'Where did you go?'

'Where were you?' I demanded in reply and started to cry.

The woman with whom Memme had been talking took me roughly by the collar and wagged a finger in my face.

'You've caused your grandmother a lot of worry and heartache. Aren't you ashamed?'

'But . . . I . . .' I wanted to explain, but not to this lady.

There were tears in Memme's eyes. She was shaking and hugging me close again. She still loved me. I loved her.

I would explain later.

21 Straight to England

In this camp, time went quickly. I didn't even get a chance to explore. There was a canal next to the camp. And a bridge with a lock. The lock opened every time a barge came through but it was a tedious business waiting for the water level to rise or fall, that it was like emptying the ocean with a spoon.

Before I got a chance to cross that bridge even, we had to pack and move on.

We were back on a train, thundering once more towards England. Which seemed even further away than ever.

I was sitting opposite Memme on the wooden bench, looking out of the window at the telegraph wires going up and down. And keeping a hand on her skirt. I was not letting her out of my sight again.

Memme had been reading one of her books but had fallen asleep. Her glasses were down on her nose and the book was slipping sideways.

This wasn't a camp train but a German public train and different. People were neat and well dressed. And so polite. The 'gentlemen' lifted their hats to say hello. And 'ladies' wore 'hairdos'. One 'gentleman' helped Memme hoist our bundles into the baggage rack. I couldn't help noticing that we were the only ones with bundles. Others had suitcases. And they kept peering at us out of the corners of their eyes. It was a bit embarrassing!

Ever since that last camp with the 'china' toilets, I was beginning to feel different. It was getting stranger and stranger just to be myself.

The man next to Memme kept staring at us! Especially at my coat. Memme had made it for me from my old fur coat, bits of grey blanket, and an old brown dress and a navy jacket.

And he was looking at my hat too. My floppy loppy! As if he'd never seen anything like it before.

The train stopped often.

The stations were nearly all bombed out but being rebuilt rapidly. There was scaffolding across the platforms and workmen were hammering between the rails.

A man came to the window selling bottles of lemonade, chocolate and kringels.

I wanted some.

Memme opened her eyes for a moment and frowned a silent 'no'!

We had no money.

A little later she asked me if I was hungry? She said we had some bread and jam with us in one of the baskets. But no one else was eating bread and jam from a basket. I said 'no' hastily. It didn't seem right.

We rode the train all day until the sun started setting. By the time it was dark, most of the people had got out. The man next to Memme moved to another seat and stretched his legs out. He had taken off his shoes, loosened his tie and had his hat over his eyes.

Memme told me to lie across the seat and rest.

Now the man wasn't watching us any more, I felt better. I asked for the bread and jam. Then settled down and slept.

Somewhere in the night. The carriage was dark. Lights were flashing by the window. Memme had her nose buried in the silver fox fur. She must have felt me wake up because she whispered, 'We're in Holland.'

I looked out of the window at Holland darkness, Holland lights. Every now and then a Holland street with matchbox square Holland houses. And some Holland ruins. The last was comforting. It tied in with who I was. Where I was going. Where I came from. I had begun to feel unreal.

Next time I woke up, the train was standing still.

I had the impression that the train was standing inside a big building.

Memme was straightening her hat pin. The 'gentleman' was lacing his shoes. He came over and helped Memme once more with the bundles. I wished he wouldn't.

Through the window I was relieved to notice that we were not the only Bundle Peters after all! There were others getting out of the train and piling their things on the platform.

Instead of soldiers or guards, men in overalls and leather caps came to help with the luggage. And some women dressed in navy uniforms with red crosses on their armbands, gathered around the bundles and took charge.

One of those women stepped into our carriage too and came straight to us. Without a word she started hoisting our things out to the platform. She was very thin with a long pointed nose. She moved quickly and abruptly and her eyes were needle sharp, like a bird's. Soon all our things were outside on one of the trolleys and a leather cap was ready to wheel them away.

'Wait,' shouted Memme. She couldn't let him take her bundles, she needed them with her all the time! But the woman didn't understand. Memme turned to the gentleman for help, but he shrugged. Said he didn't speak English, in German. He raised his hat politely and went his own way.

The woman took my hand. 'Come on child.' She grabbed Memme under the arm and marched us both towards a side door. She walked so quickly we could barely keep up with her. Memme's hat fell down and her coat buttons came undone. She would have liked to stop and fasten them.

But the woman was not going to stop yet. She was persistent. She smiled a few times to show she meant well but we must obey her. A funny person she was! Half man, half woman, and more like a machine.

She led us to a big dining room. We were going to be fed again.

There was a long table in the centre, laid with a white tablecloth and covered with shining cutlery. More silver and china! I was getting used to it already!

Other refugees were already sitting and we were told to sit too, though we were not allowed to choose our own chair but had to go where the woman put us. She stood behind us like a guard. Everybody had a visor-capped Red Cross woman standing behind them in the same way and there was not much conversation.

Memme sat down heavily, fighting for breath. But she whispered happily, 'We're going to get some real English food.'

Somewhere close, a boat's horn indicated that we were near a harbour.

I felt embarrassed again. The Red Cross women were trying to talk to us but only one woman among us spoke English. And that so badly that she got into an even bigger mess than if she couldn't speak it at all. It was hard to sit and smile and smile and have nothing to do. Some admired the cutlery. Others were rolling the edges of the tablecloth or sipping water repeatedly. The ship's horn sounded again and made us jump.

There were other children at the table. We sat tightly and tensely, like when visiting and 'on our best behaviour'.

The lady next to Memme leaned over and whispered, 'Isn't it nice to be back in civilization?'

Memme nodded.

So this was 'civilization'? No wonder it was so strange! Like another country.

The food arrived at last! It was carried to us ready served on plates. I waited for mine with anticipation. I already loved English food – the white bread and jam.

The plate appeared before me. There was a piece of something brown on it, a spoonful of white paste, three tiny tiny cabbages? I asked Memme for an explanation.

'The brown is roast beef,' she explained, 'the white mashed potatoes, and the little green cabbages are called Brussels sprouts.'

I took my first mouthful and 'Ugh!'

Memme dug me with her elbow to be quiet.

But the stuff was awful. I whispered to her that it didn't taste of anything at all. It was more like the grass soup I made for my dolls than real food. As for the 'roast beef'! My mouth was full of 'roast beef' and it wouldn't go down. I chewed and chewed but it just went round and round, like eating my boots.

I was about to spit it out when the Red Cross woman leaned over and asked us how we liked the food. At least that was what I think she asked us because Memme gave me a sign to smile and nod.

Looking round the table, I found I was not the only one who didn't like it. When no one was looking, I put my hand over my mouth and the 'roast beef' slid under the table. Followed by the Brussels sprouts.

But it wasn't the end yet. The plates were taken away and small dishes were set in their place, with a piece of brown with yellow sauce on it. I was not rushing in there this time, but tasted warily. I was glad I did. The brown was poison. But the yellow tasted good.

Memme said the brown was 'Christmas pudding', the yellow, custard.

I skimmed the yellow from the brown, re-evaluating my ideas about English food.

The meal ended with a cup of tea. With milk in it, of all things!

As we rose to leave the table, we were each given a cardboard box full of sandwiches, for later. I had already decided that when

I got to England all I was going to eat there was bread and jam and cornflakes.

The dining room led straight out to a quay. We were in a harbour. The sea air was cold and stingy and smelled of fish.

We were led up a gangplank and into a ship. Then down stairs into a big room full of bunks. In familiar surroundings again, I relaxed and remembered I was still hungry. Memme let me have a top bunk. I climbed up to eat the sandwiches, spread with sardines.

The room filled up. The ship's motors purred in the walls and the doorway belched hot oil fumes.

Memme lay down on the bunk below and started worrying about her bundles. She was completely lost without them, and felt sure she would never see them again.

I must have fallen asleep. When I opened my eyes the whole bed was shaking and the room was too. It was swaying from side to side. And I felt sick.

I called to Memme quickly, that I was going to throw up. Memme helped me to climb down and rushed me to the toilets. But they were full of people being sick already. The cubicles were locked. The floor swayed up and down. I slid forward then backwards on the vomit. The sinks were full of sick too. It wouldn't go down the plug hole.

Memme pounded on one of the cubicle doors, calling to the person inside that 'we won't be a minute'. To 'let the child come in'.

The woman inside the toilet agreed finally to let me in, but 'only for a minute'.

I slipped past her and found myself facing the toilet bowl. But it slid sideways and up towards the ceiling. I just could not catch it for long enough. The floor went with it, and it was all I could do to keep my feet! I would have liked to lie on the floor, I felt so bad.

Memme came in and helped me by holding my head. Then led me back to the bunks.

'It'll pass when we get to England,' she comforted me.

I went to lie on Memme's bunk. She removed her underskirt (bemoaning her bundles once more), sat by my feet and wiped my face with the wet skirt, rinsing it out every few minutes after I was sick.

I wasn't sea sick when we came from Estonia. It must have been the roast beef and Christmas pudding. In fact I could taste them all, the Brussels sprouts and the sardines, even after I had nothing left to be sick on.

Memme's presence was with me, in the background. She whispered reassurance. 'It won't be long now.' But the night had no meaning in time, until suddenly she asked if I wanted to go on deck.

'Is it morning?'

'Yes, and we're moving into the harbour. We're in England.'

'England.'

'The fresh air will do you good.' Memme helped me up the stairs. It was light already, and bitterly cold.

We crossed the deck to stand at the rail, in the icy wind and salt spray. 'That's England over there,' Memme pointed at some white cliffs and a grey, grey sky.

22 My First Ice Cream

As soon as we stepped on land, we were approached by yet another Red Cross woman. This one was much more a person than the first and much friendlier. She took my hand and guided us to a waiting train. Another train!

But what a train! This had to be the sort of train English kings and queens rode in. The seats were soft like couches and furry. There were beautiful lamps and thick curtains pulled back by satin tassels.

Memme thought it was special too and bounced up and down a couple of times before sitting, releasing a cloud of dust.

The Red Cross woman sat next to Memme. I sat opposite, by the window. Between us was a table, elegantly spread with a white tablecloth and with handsome silver, monogrammed 'B.R.' I wondered who B.R. was?

More roast beef? My stomach heaved at the thought, but I dared not talk to Memme while the woman was sitting with us. I pressed myself into a corner of the soft seat and was stunned by all this splendour. It had started slowly, but now it was everywhere.

The tablecloth was stiff with starch. So stiff that it shone. I daren't even touch it.

The train filled up. The passengers were talking in whispers. No one talked loudly or laughed heartily, the way people did in camps. The Red Cross lady smiled and talked to Memme but even that was a buzz-buzz. When she smiled, something was missing. She was like those tall buildings, of cold concrete. Her eyes remained vacant.

I knew people were looking at us, again, only this time not straight, but 'discreetly'. If they were caught, they looked away.

They looked through us, at our bundles and our clothes. And at the luggage tag the Red Cross woman had tied around my neck. Like I was a dog. I didn't like it. I think Memme felt that way too. She had pressed herself into the deep corner and kept fussing with her hat and collar. We were going to have tea.

A waiter in a white jacket bent over the table, and placed on it a silver tray of tea things. His eyes skimmed us with a surprised lift of an eyebrow before he went away. The Red Cross woman made a ritual of sugar passing and nodding. Memme pressed her cup to her chest and sought comfort from it. At least it gave her something to do.

I didn't want tea! I didn't want anything except to be somewhere else! I shifted even closer to the window.

The train rushed through a grey land, sometimes greyer than other times. Sometimes a sooty black. The trees and even the grass were grey. Thick clouds hung low and tiny raindrops beaded the glass.

The woman rose suddenly and went away. I was relieved. I wanted to sit next to Memme but Memme said no. She straightened her hat and forbade me to lick the teaspoon, which I felt like doing. She blinked her eyes at me a couple of times to remind me to be 'on my best behaviour'. And that, I think, summed it all up. I had been on my best behaviour ever since we had left the camps.

In the camps it had been friendly and cosy. One could laugh when one wanted to. We had all been the same. Now we were different again and it was the same old problem of being for ever different that was getting me down.

The Red Cross woman came back a few minutes later, smiling warmly. She placed a saucer of something on the table in front of me. Butter with wafers? It looked like butter. A whitish butter. But there was no knife. The woman was still smiling at me. I couldn't very well spread the butter on the wafers without a knife, could I?

'Eat,' she said and sat back in her place. I didn't know what to do. I looked to Memme for help. But she too was smiling and gave me a sign with her eyebrows to eat. They couldn't understand what I was waiting for. Couldn't they see I didn't have a knife? At home I would have dug the wafers into the butter and that would have been that. But not here in this England.

As I sat dumbly, the woman picked up one of the wafers, stuck a corner in the butter and passed it to me.

'Eat,' she said again.

I took a bite and wow! It wasn't butter at all. It was icy cold and delicious.

'Ice cream,' said the Red Cross woman.

So that's what it was! Ice cream! The woman thought it was funny that I didn't know about ice cream. She showed me how to put it between the wafers and how to lick it. It was the most wonderful thing I had eaten, except chocolate. I offered Memme some but she said she had eaten it before, in Estonia. Her voice took on that reminiscing edge of sadness with which she remembered 'her youth'.

Having found some means of communication, the Red Cross lady became almost jolly. After I had eaten the last bite and licked my fingers clean, she got up and brought more. Despite Memme's polite protestations. This time flavoured with chocolate.

When I'd finished again and Memme had drunk her tea, we were led to another carriage. Just as soft and furry but without the tablecloth on the table. The woman and Memme started filling out forms.

I felt a little freer, enough so to go and stand by the door and look out of the lowered window. The wind whipped past, tearing at my hat, and I had to hold it tightly to keep it on. The air was still thick. Little specks of soot flew up into my eyes.

I couldn't understand how everything so rich and beautiful could be dirty at the same time. Like the furry seat, when Memme bounced on it?

What kept me at the window were the red double decker buses. I had never seen anything like those buses before in my life. And they wobbled so, it was a wonder they didn't topple over!

As I was following one around a curve with my eyes and it seemed to be falling on its side, I forgot to hold my Lotu. My head was half out of the window and to my horror, I saw my loppy lotti doing a pink velvet arc and disappearing towards the sooty warehouses. Just before the train thundered into a tunnel. I had to pull my head back quick.

The loss of that hat was an awful blow. The final end to sunshine. To Inge, Cat and all my friends!

I pressed my nose against the glass and saw only my own face, mirrored in the darkness. I had to tell Memme.

But Memme was glad. She said Mimma would buy me a new one anyway, and proper clothes. I didn't need it any more, she said.

But I did need it!

I sat back in my seat, and would rather have sat on Memme's lap. Suddenly I wasn't Lotukata any more! My head felt naked. And I wasn't Rin Tin Tin either. All I had left was my real name, on the tag around my neck.

Without my hat, Inge wouldn't know me. Cat neither. I wasn't an officer any more. Just a girl, in a grey strange land.

'Civilization.' I had lost my summer woods. The warm grass between the corn fields. Warm puddles in July.

23 The End or a New Beginning

Our room was high up in this hotel, at least on the fifth floor. All the houses in London were with many storeys and most of them were joined together. A whole street could be just one building. And the streets were so tightly packed with people and cars it was a wonder anyone could get to where they were going. And there was so much noise! I couldn't sleep all night. Memme put cotton wool in her ears but I wouldn't let her put any in mine. I wanted to listen to England. It was all so very exciting.

The Red Cross lady took me and some other children for a walk. I held tightly to her hand, afraid of being swept away by the crowds. She didn't even notice them.

We passed shop windows, great big ones made of glass. There was so much clothing and furniture and food. And parks and swans and babies in high carriages with frills and laces. An 'underground' with 'escalators', I remembered the words but I was scared all the same. And I was glad when we were back on the street, with dogs on leads, high-heeled shoes and flower sellers, and 'newspaper men'. What was a newspaper, I wondered?

'Don't step on the grass!'

'Don't touch!'

One of the shop counters was so long it reached right out into the street. It was piled high, in pyramids, with oranges, apples, berries in all colours and something in a bunch, yellow and curved called 'Fyffe'. Those 'Fyffes' looked interesting, I wondered what they'd taste like?

I wanted to taste one of those 'Fyffes' the way we took things we wanted in the camp, but the man was right there, asking for money.

Now I understood what Memme had meant about grownups 'earning their bread'. I had thought they were given a loaf of bread for doing a job, but I understood now they could have either. A loaf of bread or money.

I noticed a man in uniform standing in the middle of the street. I could tell right away he was a policeman, but he didn't have a gun or a rifle. He didn't use any kind of force, yet the traffic stopped for him anyway. All he did was to put up his hand.

The bathrooms and toilets in the hotel were the same porcelain, you might like to know. With chains that send the water roaring down the toilet bowl, followed by a long hissing. I wondered how they worked? I was going to find out just as soon as I could.